women [re] build

STORIES POLEMICS FUTURES

Preface by Joan Ockman

Editors:
Franca Trubiano
Ramona Adlakha
Ramune Bartuskaite

a|r
+d

APPLIED
RESEARCH
+DESIGN
PUBLISHING

CONTENTS

ACKNOWLEDGMENTS

Projects sometimes have the unlikeliest of origins. This one began on the morning of Wednesday, November 8, 2016, when Dean Fritz Steiner of the Weitzman School of Design, so graciously met us to receive our request for financial support. We had had a fairly difficult night, having barely come to accept the results of the American presidential race. Undeterred, however, the editors of this book were thrilled by the generous support offered by Dean Steiner in pursuit of an international conference dedicated to the question of women in architecture. Then, as now, Dean Steiner has been a vocal and committed supporter of Penn Design Women in Architecture (PWIA), including his most recent advocacy for this book. Both the symposium "[Re]Form, The Framework, Fallout, and Future of Women in Design" and *Women [Re]build: Stories, Polemics, Futures* would have been impossible without his support and for this we are forever grateful. In addition, we wish to thank Winka Dubbeldam who, as chair of the Architecture Department, greatly facilitated all aspects of the symposium planning and continues to champion the role of PWIA in the Architecture Department. The staff at the Dean's Office, the Finance Office, and the Architecture office have also helped and encouraged the project.

Indeed, a project such as this involves a tremendous amount of input and assistance by others. The editors are particularly grateful for the continued intellectual support offered by Joan Ockman who was not only seminal to the organization of the symposium, but equally the inspiration for our decision to pursue the publication. Joan graciously advised us on matters of structure, design, and the book's underlying premise. For this, and for many other lessons conveyed in the process, we are very thankful. We are also thrilled that each of the authors who submitted their work for publication did so enthusiastically and without reserve. While some authors participated in the original symposium, and others did not, the diversity of voices represented in each of the four sections speaks to the merit of their ideas, experiences, scholarship, and work. Their careers have written new chapters in the history of architecture.

To Gordon Goff of Applied Research + Design (ORO Editions and Goff Books), we appreciate your eager review of the manuscript and agreeing to publish it. To Jake Anderson, who facilitated its production, we are grateful for your patience. To Andrew Saunders from Penn Design and Sean Burke associate general counsel of the University of Pennsylvania, we thank them for their advice. And finally to Sarah Holland, we thank her for her initial graphic design vision.

Ramune Bartuskaite thanks Leta Bartuska for being her first and most influential female role model and Ramunas Bartuska for his continuous love and support. To Benjamin Swofford for his never-ending encouragement and perspective. And a special thank you to professors at Miami University, especially John Humphries, Dr. Jim Friedman, and Dr. Regan Henry for helping her find her voice so she could now lift the voice of others.

Building a life filled with endless possibilities, continual encouragement, and boundless love, Ramona Adlakha would like to thank those who made this possible. To her father, Sunil, for teaching her that caring for others is the most important task of all; to her mother, Mitali for being the most inspiring example of all that a woman can be; and to her sister, Sheena for always reminding her how wonderful life can be with a sister by her side. A special thank you to architect, friend, and mentor, Larry Wayne Richards for his guidance and support.

For Franca Trubiano, this project has an even earlier beginning. When she was but six months out of architecture school. The day was December 6, when a gunman decided to target and kill fifteen women engineering students at the École Polytechnique de Montréal. The event was devastating for a number of reasons, not least of which because women were singled out for daring to study engineering—a male dominated profession. While this occurred in the city where she lived, the fact that engineering is a sister discipline to architecture was too close to ignore for herself and her graduating sisters. Within months, they had organized, named their group Geomatria, met repeatedly, and established a program of action to empower themselves. They fundraised, volunteered, renovated women's shelters, and educated themselves in ways that their 'professional' training had not. This decision to publicly confront the issue of women in architecture was transformative, and possibly a catalyst to her remaining in the profession. To all the women of Geomatria, thank you. And to Yves, Ziva, and Luca, thank you for your continued patience through yet another project.

The editors would also like to thank Rose Deng, Mary Swysgood, and Kirin Kennedy who also co-founded Penn Design Women in Architecture, as well as members Nicole Bronola, Susan Kolber, Caitlin Dashiell, Marta Llor, Aishwarya Katta, Aahana Miller, and all future Penn Design Women in Architecture. Most importantly, this book is dedicated to all the young women who imagine their futures as architects and who wonder if they can. Of course they can, and course they must.

Franca Trubiano
Ramona Adlakha
Ramune Bartuskaite

#WeToo

Preface by Joan Ockman

The symposium at the University of Pennsylvania School of Design that gave rise to this book, "[RE]Form: The Framework, Fallout, and Future of Women in Design," took place in April 2017. As it turned out, it was a pivotal moment for feminism. Six months earlier the first female candidate for the United States presidency had lost to an opponent who not only was unqualified for the job by any conventional standards but, by his own admission in a videotape that surfaced a month before the election, was a sexual predator. A year later, six months after the symposium at Penn, the #MeToo movement was born when, following revelations about the abusive behavior of a powerful Hollywood mogul, a stream of women began coming forward to add their names to a growing list of victims. The hashtag went viral as the shocking litany of exploitation came to light, from the boardroom to the locker room, from the corridors of Congress to the halls of academe, wherever men exercised their prerogatives with impunity. What was so disturbing was not just the universality of the women's trauma but the ubiquity of the misconduct. Reports of new scandals seemed to surface every week. Things came to a head in fall 2018 when a female professor agreed to give public testimony at a Congressional hearing about a nominee to the Supreme Court who, she alleged, had tried to rape her when they were in high school. The nominee prevailed, but not without a divisive and wrenching spectacle that played out on national television. Meanwhile new disclosures about hush money paid by the now sitting president shortly before the election, to a porn star and a Playboy bunny, continued to trickle out.

All of this is more than well known, yet it is worth rehearsing the chronology of events in relation to the architecture profession and, in doing so, to place the present publication into a larger picture. Oddly enough, architecture was late to the public reckoning. At another academic conference, this one held in early 2018 at Yale School of Architecture, titled "Rebuilding Architecture," the speakers in a closing panel devoted to architecture and the media responded to a question from a woman in the audience who demanded to know why architects, notorious for bad behavior toward women, had escaped being implicated in the current publicity. Reacting sympathetically, the speakers—including three seasoned journalists—expressed frustration about how difficult it was to get the story out: women architects were reluctant to go on record, fearful of the impact on their careers and the scrutiny it would bring to their personal lives. Finally, however, #MeToo found its way to architecture when, in March 2018, a reporter for the *New York Times* broke a story on the front page titled "5 Women Accuse the Architect Richard Meier of Sexual Harassment." The women interviewed described incidents spanning four decades in which the now eighty-four-year-old architect had assaulted them. The immediate result was that Meier took a leave of absence from his firm, and the New York Chapter of the AIA quickly stripped him of a 2018 design award; seven months later Meier's firm announced that his departure was permanent. Also around the time the *Times* article appeared a "Shitty Architecture Men" list—a crowdsourced spreadsheet containing allegations from anonymous accusers of sexual and other misconduct against more than 100 (and a couple women) in architecture—began circulating on the internet. Modeled on a "Shitty Media Men" list that had debuted six months earlier, the spreadsheet was intended, according to its creator, to provide those who had been subjected to harassment or discriminatory behavior in the firm or the classroom with a place to vent. It lived online for a few months before being taken down. Despite a disclaimer on the site that the content was unverified, the uncorroborated accusations and gossipy invective caused reputational damage to those who were called out and, not surprisingly, led to threatened lawsuits. But it was clear that Meier was just the tip of the iceberg.

Almost exactly four decades ago, my first job out of architecture school was in Richard Meier's office. At the time there were twenty-five or thirty employees in the firm, of which less than a handful were women. The atmosphere was, to put it euphemistically, unconvivial. The whiteness of the office, which we shared with a set of pristine architectural models, was matched by the general chilliness. Long hours were the rule, salaries were very low, and employee turnover was high. Partial compensation came from interesting work on the drawing boards, and it was possible for a young designer to learn a lot. I stayed close to my cubicle, mostly writing descriptions of buildings for a monograph Meier was preparing on his work. I was never the object of any untoward advances. However, another young woman in the office was involved in a relationship with the boss that was an open secret, and it was hard not to be distracted by it. Eight months later, when I was offered an appealing job editing architectural publications, I was happy to jump ship. This was the end of my ambition to become a practicing architect. The other woman, who remained in the office for a few more years, has a successful career today in a different field.

Who knows how many aspiring women architects have had their career plans derailed or detoured by negative professional experiences? To judge by current statistics, female attrition in architecture offices remains very high even as women's enrollment in architecture schools now just about equals men's. It's high time for women in architecture to tell their stories, whether as a form of catharsis or as a cautionary tale for upcoming colleagues. Of course, there are also positive and inspirational stories to be told, and some of them, by contemporary and historical women who have managed to beat the odds, are eloquently recounted in this book. Practical initiatives are also underway and, while painfully slow, incremental progress is being made. In September 2018, in response to lobbying efforts, the American Institute of Architects updated its Code of Ethics and Professional Conduct, explicitly addressing matters of sexual harassment, equity in the profession, and sustainability. The professional ecosystem now also includes so-called sanctuary firms, offering alternative kinds of work environments. The silver lining of the experience of the last few years, with all its dramatic developments and appalling revelations, is a newly emboldened and conscious feminist movement, and more sophisticated pushback against the status quo. The demand for change appears to be sweeping up women in architecture as well. *We too.*

Joan Ockman
March 2019

BUILDING OUR VOICE

Ramona Adlakha & Ramune Bartuskaite

A little over three years ago, as is typical of the architecture student's experience, we found ourselves engaged in a rather spirited discussion on the pros and cons of our first completed year of graduate school. Having both worked at design firms before enrolling in the Master of Architecture program at the University of Pennsylvania, we chatted about the vastly different lives we had led prior to graduate school. We were keenly aware of the differences in our experiences as young designers working at a firm versus graduate students in architecture, and just how much our worlds had shifted from being employed in the field to pursuing our academic endeavors. Graduate school opened up a world of opportunities, many of which were not as apparent in the workplace. Speaking with classmates, we realized that our views resonated with many of our female peers who had worked in the field before going back to school. It was not lost on us that while a fifty/fifty distribution of men and women existed in our graduate school, in the field only thirty-two percent of practitioners are female, and a mere seven percent are in positions of leadership (as reported in our Equity by Design article by Annelise Pitts). Why have these metrics of women students not carried over to the profession? What is happening between graduation and licensure that leads to the decline of women practicing architecture? This disparity between the academic world and the working environment is an issue we became interested to understand further. Moreover, why did our years as undergraduate students in design programs not prepare us for the demands and inherent biases of the workplace? Would our graduate education better prepare us? What could we do to ensure this?

As noted, there was no quantitative gender disparity at school, yet the skills and tools required to thrive at work were fundamentally missing from our graduate education. Those of us who had previously worked in the field understood the challenges that women faced in the profession. We were concerned that there were too few female architects to look up to and learn from. The few practicing role models we attained over the years struggled on their journeys to the top. Given available statistical evidence, our firsthand experiences, and the stories we heard from our colleagues, it became clear that women in architecture were not getting the recognition, respect, and opportunities for advancement as quickly as their male counterparts. We learned the working environment was not accommodating to women with children and families, often forcing them to choose between excelling at work and spending time with their loved ones. Too few firms allowed for the flexibility to excel in both. This is concerning, for architectural excellence can only be as good as the diverse body of people who practice it. By not providing equal opportunities to support the fifty percent of female graduate students, we face the risk of losing a tremendously talented, strong, and dedicated workforce who could greatly contribute to the advancement of our field.

Our academic environment provided us the support and tools to do well in design studios and lectures, and we were taught by admirable female and male professors. The struggles and challenges faced in school were faced by us all, no matter our gender. Yet, we knew this would not be the case in the field. Our positive educational experiences made us even more interested to learn if there was a way to bridge both our academic and professional worlds, and if so, could it better prepare us for our future? What were some steps we could take to ensure we had an equal role to play, a story to tell, a job to fulfill once we graduated? The answer was simple: cultivating leadership and fostering a community in which every voice would be heard.

Like all disaster preventative measures, in the fall of 2016, five friends came together to form what is now known as PennDesign Women in Architecture. We made it our mission to engage our colleagues, our community, and our extended network to collaborate and cultivate leadership, by eliminating the divide between our workplace and our education.

Fully aware that we would one day leave the school environment and enter the workforce as a competent force to be reckoned with, if the educational environment would not prepare us for the potential challenges that we would face upon graduation, we felt inclined to take matters into our own hands. Together with our classmates, colleagues, professors, and professional connections, we set out to mobilize a community of designers and thinkers with the purpose of increasing the visibility and voice of women in architecture. We wanted to understand the challenges that drive women out of the profession and what steps we could take to prevent this from happening to us. Our hope was to bring awareness to the gender disparity that exists in the profession and empower each other by fostering growth, promoting the success of women architects, and above all, cultivating the next generation of leaders in the industry. The organization fundraised to further the group's mission, and organized countless firm crawls across the Northeast of the United States to better gauge various working environments and expand our professional networks. We organized two widely attended symposia and launched a continually expanding mentorship program. As students, we joined local professional organizations to better understand the needs of a young, female architecture workforce. We provided a platform for both students and professionals to discuss and debate the topic of Women in Architecture in workshops and training sessions, which equipped participants with tools and strategies for taking ownership of their careers. Happily enough, the group's success can be measured in that for every achievement attained, two more opportunities for success emerged. This was due in large part to the support and camaraderie we received. Building this platform of women leaders not only fostered in us deep friendships but also a vast network of supporters. We learned that for every woman's success, there are five other women rooting for her. Our interest is not in self-promotion but in celebrating our peers. And hence, integral to our mission is to document the ideas and achievements of our fellow female colleagues, much of which is found in this compendium of work. Our female role models, professors, architects, activists, and builders have made significant strides by pushing against the boundaries of gender inequality and addressing the important issues which continue to define our careers. By offering this publication, we hope to bring forward their work while contributing to the movement for a more equitable future.

We strongly believe that leadership begins when we each take responsibility and accountability for our actions, serving as enablers working to empower and continually inspire each other. We are lucky to belong to a profession that is rich in creativity and boundless in possibility. We are excited to contribute our efforts to furthering our profession and we hope to be active participants in the continual cultivation of leadership, storytelling, and a more equitable playing field. Whether working at the scale of a city, a residential home, an academic paper, a conference, in a classroom, or in politics, we are women in architecture and we have many stories to tell.

HOW WILL WE KNOW
WHEN, AND IF, WOMEN HAVE [RE]BUILT ARCHITECTURE?

Franca Trubiano

The question of how it is that we will know when women have truly succeeded in transforming architecture, and its allied practices of design and construction, is both a simple question and one near impossible to answer. How will we know if women who participate in the art, craft, discipline, theory, and business of architecture—as students, educators, amateurs, professionals, critics, or clients—have achieved the level of parity, transformation, and revolution they desire? What evidence will we use to identify, measure, or evaluate appreciable gains, improvements, and added value in the status of women in architecture? More critically, is our concern with parity and representational fairness an appropriate goal?

Undoubtedly, the number of women who study, work, and teach in architecture, landscape architecture, urban design, and industrial design continues to increase with every year. In architecture, for example, many universities boast near gender parity amongst their student population. According to published data by the Association of Collegiate Schools of Architecture (ACSA), in 2014 an equal number of women and men were attending and graduating from accredited schools of architecture.[1] Moreover, the same percentage of women (forty percent) reported registering for the professional licensing exam, that is the Architectural Registration Exam.[2] In general, there is much to be optimistic given these changing demographics. Moreover, examples abound of increased efforts to facilitate the introduction and acclimation of women to the profession. In the United States, for example, the American Institute of Architects—a voluntary professional organization that oversees to the architect's continuing education and her involvement in a wide range of public policy issues associated with the built environment—hosts a number of initiatives specifically tailored to women. In 2015, the Women's Leadership Summit registered 300 participants who gathered to discuss persistent professional challenges and barriers faced by women in practice.[3] The summit succeeded in publishing the "Diversity in the Profession of Architecture" report, which gathered data and observations made by more than 7,500 architects. Job satisfaction, reasons for leaving the profession, methods for attracting women and underrepresented minorities, and factors which make architecture less than attractive as a profession were all subjects queried by the report. In 2019, Minneapolis, Minnesota, will host another Women's Leadership Summit whose goals are to "raise the profile of women in the profession; explore new paths to leadership; create a learning environment that supports the needs of multiple career stages in one event; [and] provide a space for women architects to learn from one another."[4] Local chapters of AIA Women in Architecture Committees are found in New York City, Philadelphia, Palm Beach, Miami, Chicago, Boston, Kansas City, and Richmond. And an "AIA Women in Architecture Tool Kit" exists for helping women launch their own local chapter.[5] At present, there is much energy and commitment on the part of the AIA to empower its women membership and to increase the representation of women within the profession.

And yet, as reported in a set of statistics offered in a panel at the 2016 AIA Convention, "Establishing the Business Case for Women in Architecture," forty-five percent of architecture graduates were women and thirty-five percent of AIA members held Associate status, but only eighteen percent of full members were women and only seventeen percent of senior management (partner or principal) in AIA registered architecture firms were women.[6] Hence, notwithstanding significant efforts and investments during the past two decades in strengthening the professional development of women, little has substantially changed in what concerns the participation of women in senior, mission critical, executive, and political spheres of the discipline. While some gains have certainly been registered, systemic changes are far fewer and less evident.

Women [Re]Build: Stories, Polemic, Futures was conceived in response. The ambition of this edited book is to increase the visibility and voice of women who every day challenge the definition and practice of architecture. *Women [Re]Build* gathers words, projects, and polemics advanced by leading thinkers, activists, designers, and builders who have dared to ask, "where are the women?" Where are the women whose architectural work should be celebrated and recognized for its courage and impact; who have cultivated female leadership while challenging the very principles of the discipline they represent; and who've asked the most difficult and rigorous of questions of those who build their visions? In response, *Women [Re]Build* gathers articles and interviews that highlight the contribution of women in academia, activism, and practice. The book is organized according to four conceptual categories; the first section, Framing Stories, engages both intellectual histories and contemporary debates surrounding women's participation in architecture; Shaping Polemics offers evidence of the impact and contributions made by women who actively challenge the discipline, its definition, and its practices; Building Futures captures both the words and work of practitioners who've endeavored to build their visions, and to leave physical and cultural traces of their making; and Voices is a collection of four interviews and conversations, which feature insights from acclaimed and award-winning architects who, in their own voice, speak to their professional development and their ethics of building.

But even more broadly, the project has given rise to a fundamental reassessment of the terms of feminism in the early twenty-first century. It has encouraged many of its participants to ask whether the focus on measuring parity in matters of professional visibility, voice, acclaim, and awards is at all necessary, desirable, or appropriate? Is gauging success via quantitative benchmarks essential for answering the question, "How will we know?" Are numerical metrics of performance the only way of evaluating whether women have achieved a greater sense of value in their practice as architects, both personally and publicly? According to Ila Berman in her article "Beyond Equality: Re-gendering Architectural Education," this is entirely the wrong position to hold. To propose that women must seek performance equivalencies as defined by traditionally male dominated professions is anathema to the pursuit at hand. Rather, what is needed is the ability to challenge the very definitions, codes, and laws (whether implicit or otherwise) associated with enterprises that have excluded the participation of women for hundreds of years. Predicated on a close reading of third-wave feminism, Berman asserts that in order to truly reinvent the architect's education "we must first exorcise the essential white male subject implanted within each of us."[7] In this context, transformation is less a question of numbers and more an issue of revisiting values, visions, and ethics.

This is precisely the message shared by Jeanne Gang and Margaret Cavenagh of Studio Gang who—in addition to their commitment to gender parity in all manner of hiring and leadership—have devoted firm resources to promoting work/life balance, a sense of community, and 'actionable idealism.' They've actively challenged the very limits of their actions as professionals. In "Practice Makes Progress," Gang and Cavenagh discuss their re-framing of architectural programs, how they welcome the public into their design process, and how they facilitate the creation of social networks; all, with the goal of redefining the values and ethics of design. In service to improving the lives of others, Studio Gang believes that benefits accrue in the process of active dialogue. After all "having conversations where everyone is truly heard and encouraged to contribute—[is] a key part of building relationships, especially across differences."[8] To share is to gain, and this is a view equally held by Shirley Blumberg, founding partner of Kuwabara Payne McKenna Blumberg (KPMB) Architects. As Recipient of the Order of Canada for her contributions to the field, Blumberg has chartered a distinguished career dedicated to community building and the building of communities. With a view to improving student life, encouraging sustainability, and addressing social justice, her projects are designed and predicated on the values of inclusiveness and diversity. Facilitating access to affordable housing, to public literacy, and to university education are the hallmarks of successful societies, and in the case of Blumberg, her practice has sought to do more for the public good by spending less of its public's purse. This is a basic tenet of the architect's social contract and in "Building a New Model," Blumberg invites us to "believe [that] architecture must be a powerful tool for positive change in society." This is when "a 'model' becomes a 'movement.'"[9]

Indeed, architects often find themselves involved in highly contested matters, operating on the frontlines of social justice. The right to affordable housing, for example, is one such issue which Julie Moskovitz addresses head-on in professional practice. For decades, the return of wealth, investment, and speculation to Manhattan has placed at risk the very possibility of middle-income earners making the city their home. The survival of many an artist's loft—the signature housing type of New York City—is, at present, threatened with extinction. Engaging in political action to protect the rights of those who have lived in these buildings for decades, Moskovitz describes an alternate form of professional service of great value to a public client. In the article "In Defense of New York's Loft Law, Affordable Housing for All," Moskovitz informs the reader that sometimes the most important thing an architect can do is to become politicized on issues that matter to her. Ensuring someone can remain in their home, and staving off the forces of unbridled gentrification is one such issue. So too is ensuring a woman's access to the spaces of reproductive freedom. The textual production and activism of architect Lori Brown directs our attention to the highly disputed spatial geographies that are abortion clinics, women's shelters, and hospitals. In the twenty-first century, a woman's right to control her own body is still a source of political conflict and in her article "Status Quo," Brown identifies the many ways architecture and the built environment continue to be gendered and far from equally accessible. For many women, safe access to health services, the right to shelter, and the right to a political voice are daily struggles.

In some cases, however, working at the margins of the discipline may offer access to rare and all-important lessons and opportunities. This has been the case for Nicole Dosso who, as architect and Lead Technical Coordinator of the new World Trade Center in Manhattan, was directly involved with one of the most complex building structures erected in the United

States for more than a decade. Working at Skidmore, Owings and Merrill (SOM), she has spent a far greater amount of time than most architects on building sites, both dangerous and exhilarating. In doing so, she has been the recipient of encounters both welcome and uncomfortable, both instructive and contentious. As Dosso recounts in "Beyond the Corporate Ladder," women make up less than nine percent of the construction industry, and as such continue to face health and safety risks not encountered by their male counterparts— including discrimination and harassment. "Women are not only outnumbered in the architectural profession but are also faced with dealing with the challenge of being outnumbered as women in construction."[10] Precisely because so few women are 'seen' on construction sites is it all the more important that we celebrate their presence, even as they occupy the so-called margins of the discipline, that is construction. And, by being visible on site, women further resist the proliferation of outmoded ideas that they don't build.

In fact, whether in the numbers measured or in the beliefs altered, women and their 'representations' are crucial to transforming the culture of architecture. The greater the numbers the more the practice of architecture will be more amenable to, and mimetic of, the way women think and experience the built environment. Surely, representations are central to the very definition of architecture; for architecture is nothing if not the art of depicting design ideas via drawings, models, and words. Demonstrating, imaging, and making appear that which does not yet exist is the architect's remit. However, in the case of women, the architectural task is twofold. Not only are they called upon to create the work of architecture, but their very presence makes manifest an act of creation. In the figure of the woman who designs and builds, the muse becomes the maker. In this, architecture is doubly transformed. It is altered by the work, and it is altered by she who delivers the work. This is the promise of consequential change made possible by the participation of women in architecture. Much to our benefit, never has there been a more influential moment in the history of the arts when women have had greater control over what and how one contributes to the narrative that is architectural design. And, it is of great importance to this book that we identify, catalog, and critique the various ways that the present generation of celebrated women architects have given shape and matter to meaning.

Hence, whether we turn our attention to the widely admired Seattle Art Museum Olympic Sculpture Park, Hunter's Point South Waterfront Park, the Brooklyn Botanic Garden Visitor Center, the Krishna P. Singh Center for Nanotechnology, or the Novartis Office Building, at the center of each project completed by Marion Weiss of Weiss/Manfredi is the desire to represent the shared values of good design and the ways in which they foster a better way of life. As Weiss communicates in "Converging Horizons," in the space between buildings and landscape architecture, important narratives manifest. At one scale, the poetics of water can be shaped to express its retention and purification: at another, entire settings can be designed to evoke powerful ideas "from the picturesque to the systemic, from the territorial to the intimate."[11] In the work of Billie Tsien, similarly inspired sensibilities can be found. Her own predilection for narratives permeates the whole of her collaborative practice with partner Tod Williams. In "Partnerships in Practice," Tsien discusses the immense responsibility in offering institutions culturally significant buildings, communicative of their values. Whether we call to mind the copper-bronze alloy façade of the former Folk-Art Building in New York City, the limestone that was quarried from the Negev desert for the Barnes Foundation façade in Philadelphia, or the custom green glazed bricks hung on Skirkanich Hall at the University of Pennsylvania, materials are given life and formed in service to the expression of ideas of civic importance. In this sense, no more overwhelming a project might there be than the design of the presidential library commemorating America's first African-American president; precisely the task which Tsien faces in completing the Barack Obama Presidential Library. She acknowledges how "the values represented" in this building—meant to last a minimum of 250 years—"are terrifically important."[12] Surely, this is an understatement.

More than ever, fostering the values of hope, equity, and justice for all is important in 2019. Not to reflect upon this historical moment and on the impact women have had on the discipline and profession would be nothing short of negligent. Failing to recognize that much has changed in the gender profile of builders, designers, and architects is less than fair to the accomplishments of so many women who have struggled to claim their seat at the table of change. Certainly, a great deal of work remains to be done, but any rigorous review of the history of how women have participated in the arts, architecture, and humanities reveals an important body of scholarship in support of a new intellectual horizon. In Mary Mcleod's "The Rise and Fall and Rise Again (?) of Feminist Architecture History," the reader travels through three decades of ground-breaking publications that have rescued many a woman creator from the darkness of neglect. No longer invisible and contested, their contributions to the history of design, architecture, and philosophy are now recognized and celebrated. Captured in the words of Betty Friedan, Kate Millet, Juliet Mitchell, Dolores Hayden, Gwendolyn Wright, Hélène Cixous, Luce Irigaray, Julia Kristeva, Jennifer Bloomer, Beatriz Colomina, Catherine Ingraham, Margaret Crawford, Zeynep Çelik, Mabel Wilson, and many others, are the seminal texts which have reshaped how we think about making—be they texts or works of architecture. Decades of convincing argumentation succeeded in the "widespread acceptance of feminist concerns."[13] And yet, McLeod is clear to ring the bells of distress on two counts; the first warns women of the all-too-easy tendency to participate in "reductive charges of sexism and victimization and simplistic value judgments of good and bad"[14] in what concerns past scholarship; the second reminds us that what is won at large cost, is easily lost. The flurry of scholarship which took place between 1985 and 2000 "marked an end point—or so it seemed for nearly fifteen years—of feminism's visibility in American architecture. The flood of publications nearly ground to a halt; few schools continued to offer classes on 'gender and architecture.'"[15]

And hence, when will we know? When will we have said and changed all that we need to change ensuring that young women no longer need to ask "where are all the women architects?" When will we have managed to ensure a fair playing ground where equal efforts are given equal treatment? And when will we know that we no longer need to fear the erasure of women's voices, sentiments, and values? Hopefully soon, but we're not quite there. As Despina Stratigakos cautions in her text "Unforgetting Women Architects: A Confrontation with History and Wikipedia," the struggle to ensure that a woman's work and presence are not erased from the annals of history, is constant. Vigilance is required at all times. In her thrilling account of premeditated efforts to expunge the presence of women architects on Wikipedia, Stratigakos shocks us into realizing that many a "Der Krommodore, who identifie[s] himself as a Bavarian interested in linguistics as well as a monarchist and cigar-smoking, cognac-swilling insomniac,"[16] may be lurking in the recesses of the Internet ready to hack into the history of women in architecture. But surely, it is far less comical when the attempts to intimidate women are more personal, if not violent and illegal. Recent mediatized events in film, television, art, dance, and journalism continue to reveal that most large institutions, professions, and corporations have yet to acknowledge the systematic discrimination and intimidation of the women who work amongst their ranks; a failure which only further precipitates the loss of women who are represented in the positions of responsibility, leadership, and dare we say—power. This reality, seemingly difficult to see is, however, very much felt and present by design. In Joan Ockman's "#WeToo," architects are called out for their past and present attempts to challenge a woman's right to participate in the discipline, whether implicitly or explicitly; whether by intimidation, harassment, belittling, or attempts to silence. In a manner both intimate and lucid, Ockman speaks to the salient concerns of the #MeToo movement and their impact on those who aspire to become architects. This latest awakening in the political horizon of women and their allies has galvanized the world, further reinforcing their conviction to freely occupy all spaces of engagement—be they public, professional, or political.

So, did they know? Did the women of the Bauhaus think they had little to fear when they were admitted into the inaugural class of the new school in Weimar? Did they assume that all past struggles for intellectual, professional, and political emancipation were now over? That this book is being published on the hundredth anniversary of the founding of the Bauhaus is not lost on this author. The year that was 1919, was a propitious year, indeed. The war to end all wars was finally over. The boys were back and democracy was on the rise. Germany may have been humiliated on the battle field, but women were granted the right to vote in 1918. In 1919, Weimar's National Assembly had no less than thirty-seven women who held seats, with ninety percent of the female population having cast a vote.[17] The optimism advanced at the Bauhaus was no less categorical. The promise of a new era was palpable to anyone who attended and visited the school. After four long years of physical and material challenges, the luxury of re-imagining the education of the artist/builder was intoxicating. And by some accounts, the Bauhaus was a truly emancipated school. Men and women were both admitted into the first year. Indeed, according to Ulrike Müller in *Bauhaus Women: Art, Handicraft, Design* more women than men applied for admission during the first-year.[18] In the immediate aftermath of the war, it was not uncommon in many disciplines, industries, and on numerous work sites for women to continue to vie for positions typically filled by men, prior to their being sent to war. As such, it was not entirely surprising, that the inaugural class of students at the Bauhaus had a remarkable number of women. Even the ratio of women to men faculty members was far better than some schools of architecture today; more than thirteen percent of the faculty were women at Weimar, seventeen percent when it relocated to Dessau, and close to eight percent when the school was closed in Berlin.[19] Gunta Stölzl was the first woman Master who studied at the Bauhaus in 1919, and who participated under all three administrations, leaving only in 1931.[20] In many ways this was a veritable, radical new Garden of Eden, a twentieth-century Arcadia destined to reconcile many an otherwise

FIGURE 1. The weavers on the Bauhaus staircase. Pictured from top to bottom: Gunta Stölzl, Grete Reichardt, Ljuba Monastirskaya, Otti Berger, Elisabeth Müller, Lis Beyer, Rosa Berger, Lene Bergner, Ruth Hollos or Lore Leudesdorff, and Elisabeth Oestreicher. Photography by T. Lux Feininger. Courtesy of Bauhaus-Archiv Berlin. © Estate of T. Lux Feininger.

FIGURE 2. Schlemmer, Oskar (1888-1943). Bauhaus Stairway, 1932. Oil on canvas, 63 7/8 x 45" Gift of Philip Johnson. © The Museum of Modern Art/Licensed by SCALA / Art Resource, NY

un-productive dialectic. Not only was the school on the way to achieving near gender parity, the architect's education was saved from the polarization of art and technology, craft and industry, and matter and spirit. In the synthesis of painting, weaving, metal smiting, graphic design, theater design, ceramics, and furniture making, all sensibilities could be re-united in service to rebuilding the integrated house of art, craft, and industry that nineteenth-century academicians had so successfully undermined. This was the heady climate of change, in which the work of Gertrud Grunow, Anni Albers, Margarete Heymann-Loebenstein-Marks, Marguerire Friedlaender-Widenhain, Lilly Reich, Marianne Brandt, and Lucia Moholy came to light.[21]

Why, therefore, did the optimism of those early years quickly give way to segregated studios and workshops? Why were the women of the Bauhaus encouraged to choose the designated 'women's class,' and forgo apprenticing alongside their male counterparts?[22] Why had so many talented women been ushered into the arts of weaving, bookbinding, and pottery making?[23] And why, when women were considered for possible admission into more materially challenging classes—so perceived by the men on the faculty—was their experience and capacities undervalued compared to that of their male colleagues?[24] The story of metal artist Johanna Hummel, who applied to attend the Bauhaus is emblematic of the less than equal treatment received by these aspiring artists. As recounted by Anja Baumhoff, Hummel was informed in a letter by Walter Gropius that she would need to study "under the guidance of" her new master Naum Slutzky, even though she had submitted a fairly articulate portfolio of past work.[25] The fact that her master "had not yet passed his craft guild master's examination and was technically speaking at a similar standard to the journeywoman Hummel," did not seem to alter their evaluation of her skills.[26] Hummel refused to attend the Bauhaus. Surely, she was not the only woman to have been disappointed. Notwithstanding the school's stated interest in the wholesale transformation of architectural education, and its initial promise to host the design development of women, other than Lillie Reich—who was undoubtedly considered an interior designer in the eyes of most of her male colleagues—no woman who graduated or taught at the Bauhaus was ever considered a practicing 'Architect.'[27] Within three years of having opened its doors, the majority of women students were affiliated with the weaving workshop—the most 'female' and intimate of the material arts.

Lest we think, however, this was tantamount to being relegated to purgatory, it was not. The weaving studio at the Bauhaus was home to prolific and accomplished women. Gertrud Arndt, Marianne Gugg, Otti Berger, Michiko Yamawaki, Grette Reichardt, and Benita Koch-Otte were amongst the cohort of weavers whose handiwork opened up a new trajectory for modern art. Although some scholars have characterized their work as that of handmaidens to their male 'form masters'—Johannes Itten, Paul Klee, Wassily Kandisky, and László Moholy-Nagy—it is undeniable that as artists in their own right, these women assimilated the lessons of early modernism in the warp and weft of threads and knots.[28] As 'painters' working with linen, silk, wool, cotton, and chenille, the Bauhaus weavers composed using color, texture, thickness, and tone. Their representations abstracted landscapes, topographies, patterns—or nothing at all. Why, therefore, do we know far too little of the historiography of the pieces produced during the early years of the workshop? Maybe, because, although all workshop products were handmade they were sold without attribution and under the Bauhaus brand.[29] In this environment, evidence of the mind and hand of the weaver was sublimated in service to the larger desires of the school. Somehow it was assumed that there was little need to name, identify, and represent the vision and skill of the women who had designed and made these textile works of art.[30] One wonders how many pieces of recognizable art have been forever lost to history. How many pieces were never celebrated and cataloged? How many pieces never served to honor the young career of a weaver? And, how little opportunity there must have been for a weaver to learn from one's successes and failures? Exceptions existed of course. The leadership of Gunta Stölzl was a bright spot for women weavers in the history of the Bauhaus, and all the more remarkable because she helped transition the workshop to industrial production when it moved to Dessau in 1926.[31]

Equally bright were the beginnings of Anni Albers who arrived at the Bauhaus in 1922 and who went on to become one of the school's most accomplished weavers. It is not entirely clear whether she was interested in studying architecture and was discouraged to do so. She did state, as reported by Ulrike Müller, that "I considered weaving too womanish. I was looking for the right occupation and so I began weaving without any great enthusiasm, as this choice caused the least comment."[32] It may not have been her first choice, but it was a wise choice. In the weaving workshops of the Bauhaus, Albers began a prolific career dedicated to transforming the craft of weaving into an art. Amongst her early accomplishments was the fabric she developed for the German Trade Union—touted as having performance characteristics of light reflectivity and sound absorption.[33] And she was made the deputy head of the weaving workshop for a brief period in 1929.[34] In service to her art of the thread, Albers studied formal design with Klee, Kandisky, and Itten, for which it might be said that in collaboration with these painterly artists she developed her early design sensibilities. And during her time at the Bauhaus, she was honored with the commission to weave the tapestries gracing the Dessau home of director and wife, Walter and Ise Gropius.[35]

Amongst the period's countless victims of anti-Semitism, Albers and her husband chose to emigrate to the United States in 1933; and, thankfully, with the help of friends, between 1934 and 1949 Albers ran the weaving workshop at Black Mountain College, in North Carolina.[36] That her many fabrics, wall hangings, and tapestries were works of art, is obvious. Her recent retrospective at the Tate Modern in London is evidence enough of this fact with 350 separate pieces on view for this event.[37] What is less remembered, however, is the fact that Albers was also an accomplished writer. Throughout her career she wrote alongside her weaving. She expressed her visions both in text and thread. In 1938 she published "Work with Material" and "Weaving at the Bauhaus"; in 1942 she wrote "On Jewelry"; and in 1947 she completed "Design Anonymous and Timeless."[38] As late as 1982, she wrote "Material as Metaphor." Her books include *On Designing* published in 1957 and *On Weaving* from 1965. So eloquently described by T'ai Smith in her recent book *Bauhaus Weaving Theory–From Feminine Craft to Mode of Design*, it was in the latter book that Albers gave voice to a truly structural and material definition of weaving. As Smith argues, it was at the Bauhaus that Albers would have been introduced to workshops which, "investigated the limits of specific materials—like thread, clay, or celluloid and light—and tools—like looms, pottery wheels, or cameras—to grasp and articulate the principal elements of each craft."[39] Attention to the 'thingness' of making, to the materials and tools of her craft was essential to lifelong ambitions for her practice. Recognition of the constructed nature of the weave is what ensured Albers's position amongst the greatest modern artists of her time. Craft and design were inextricably bound in all of her works.[40] She reinvented the weaver's art in re-building its relationship to matter, technique, function, and performance. No longer the mere recipient of pictorial content, woven works of art were rebuilt at their very core. In her hands, this otherwise manual, physical, and craft-based practice—traditionally the labor of women—became a work of art. In this way, Albers rebuilt the idea and practice of weaving. She may have begun with little enthusiasm for weaving, but in the end, she left the world an intellectual legacy—what was once marginal was now central. Between the arts of painting and those of architecture, Albers positioned weaving as pictorially complex and structurally reconsidered. This she accomplished, at the loom and beyond. By weaving and writing, Albers rebuilt our understanding of the practice and theory of threads, knots, fabrics, carpets, and tapestries. We should all aspire to do the same with architecture.

Women [Re]Build: Stories, Polemic, Futures has similar aims. It has gathered into one publication, the voices and visions of women who have undoubtedly struggled to collect their histories and debate their theories, who have resisted hegemonic powers and actively tried to impact the public arena, and who have challenged the most recalcitrant of industries that is building in order to masterfully construct their dreams. There is still a great deal of doing and thinking yet to accomplish, and it may be our very destiny that we will never know, when, and if, women have re[built] architecture. No matter, it will surely not stop us from trying.

Endnotes

1   Lian Chikako Chang, "Where Are the Women? Measuring Progress on Gender in Architecture," October 2014, accessed March 18, 2019, http://www.acsa-arch.org/resources/data-resources/women.
2   Ibid.
3   Caitlin Reagan, "Women architects carving themselves a space," October 5, 2015, https://www.aia.org/articles/836-women-architects-carving-themselves-a-spacee.
4   Women's Leadership Summit, AIA, accessed April 1, 2019, https://www.aia.org/resources/180571-womens-leadership-summit.
5   Women in Architecture Toolkit, AIA October 24, 2013, accessed March 18, 2019, https://issuu.com/aiadiv/docs/women_in_architecture_toolkit.
6   Steve Cimino, "Diversity: Not a 'women-only problem,'" May 27, 2016, accessed April 1, 2019, https://www.aia.org/articles/13086-diversity-not-a-women-only-problem:26. These statistics were reported during the session by Kate Schwennsen, FAIS, based on date from the National Architectural Accrediting Board (NAAB), National Council of Architectural Registration Boards(NCARB), and the AIA.
7   See page 35 of *Women [Re]Build: Stories, Polemics and Futures*.
8   Ibid., 131.
9   Ibid., 104.
10   Ibid. 112.
11   Ibid., 23.
12   Ibid., 95.
13   Ibid., 46.
14   Ibid., 49.
15   Ibid., 46.
16   Ibid., 54.
17   Sturm, Reinhard (2011). "Weimarer Republik, Informationen zur politischen Bildung, Nr. 261 (German)," Bonn: Bundeszentrale für politische Bildung. ISSN 0046-9408. Retrieved June 17, 2013, https://en.wikipedia.org/wiki/Weimar_National_Assembly#cite_note-BPB-4.
18   Ulrike Müller, *Bauhaus Women: Art, Handicraft, Design* (Paris: Flammarion, 2009), 9.
19   Rachel, Epp Buller, Review of, "Bauhaus Women: Art, Handicraft, Design by Ulrike Müller," *Woman's Art Journal* 31, no. 2 (Fall/Winter 2010): 55-57.
20   Anja Baumhoff, "Gunta Stölzl," in *Bauhaus*, eds. Jeannine Fiedler and Peter Feierabend (Cologne: Könemann, 1999), 346-353.
21   Anja Baumhoff, "Women at the Bauhaus–a Myth of Emancipation," in *Bauhaus*, eds. Jeannine Fiedler and Peter Feierabend (Cologne: Könemann, 1999), 96-107.
22   Ibid., 102.
23   Ibid.
24   The important, but rarely acknowledged, contribution made by Lucia Moholy's photography in early years of the Bauhaus is another noteworthy example. See Rose-Carol Washton Long, "Lucia Moholy's Bauhaus Photography and the Issue of the Hidden Jew," *Woman's Art Journal* 35, no.2 (Fall-Winter 2014): 37-46
25   Ibid., 107.
26   Ibid.
27   Müller, *Bauhaus Women*, 104-111. See also Carmen Espegel, *Women Architects in the Modern Movement* (New York: Routledge, 2018), 136-163.
28   Müller, *Bauhaus Women*, 34-35.
29   Anja Baumhoff, "The Weaving Workshop," in *Bauhaus*, eds. Jeannine Fiedler and Peter Feierabend (Cologne: Könemann, 1999), 471.
30   Ibid.
31   Ibid, 472-473.
32   Müller, *Bauhaus Women*, 104-11. See also Carmen Espegel, *Women Architects in the Modern Movement* (New York: Routledge, 2018), 52.
33   Baumhoff, "The Weaving Workshop," 475.
34   Ibid.
35   Müller, *Bauhaus Women*, 104-11. See also Carmen Espegel, *Women Architects in the Modern Movement* (New York: Routledge, 2018), 52.
36   Müller, *Bauhaus Women*, 53.
37   "Tate Modern Exhibition: Anni Albers," Tate Modern, accessed April 1, 2019, https://www.tate.org.uk/whats-on/tate-modern/exhibition/anni-albers.
38   "Selected Writings – Anni Albers," The Josef & Anni Albers Foundation, accessed April 1, 2019, https://albersfoundation.org/artists/selected-writings/anni-albers/#tab2.
39   T'ai Smith, *Bauhaus Weaving Theory – From Feminine Craft to Mode of Design* (Minneapolis, MN: University of Minnesota Press, 2014), xiii.
40   Ibid., xvii.

CONVERGING HORIZONS

HORIZONS

AN INTERVIEW WITH MARION WEISS

Marion Weiss was the keynote speaker at Penn Design's 2017 Women in Architecture symposium "[RE]Form: The Framework, Fallout, and Future of Women in Design." Following the event, she was interviewed by Ramona Adlakha and Ramune Bartuskaite, who asked Marion to further discuss some of the major points she made during her presentation regarding her background, experience, and hopes for the future of women in the field of design.

Q When did you decide that you wanted to study architecture and to be an architect?

A As a child, I had parallel dreams of being a concert pianist, film director, and an architect. While I was mostly focused on becoming a concert pianist, I was also inspired by our Danish uncle—really a close family friend—who designed modernist homes on the steep hillsides of the Bay Area in California, where I grew up. His collection of *Habitat* publications inspired me to build a series of doll houses—really more like stackable modules—that could be configured to shape linear parks, define courtyard housing, or become high rise towers. By seventh grade I had built twenty-one units. Parallels between music and architecture are endless, but my own experience has made me appreciate the enduring impact that form—both explicit and implicit—can have to support infinite freedom and creative expression.

Q Shortly after winning the Women's Memorial competition in 1989, you were quoted in the *Los Angeles Times* regarding the experience of women in the profession, as stating, "I wish I could say it was easier, but it is difficult for women to get ahead…I'm optimistic that there are more and more role models for women." Do you think things are different now? To that end, do you identify yourself as a "feminist"? If so, how?

A Things are profoundly different now. The number of women doing extraordinary and inspiring work has grown with intensity and, in part, this is because the media has brought visibility to their work. You could argue that the media was less interested in their accomplishments before, and there were fewer opportunities for them to achieve legible impact. And feminism, effectively, articulates the agency and capacity women have to lead and invent.

Q You have been a longstanding faculty member at Penn Design. What else have you taught in addition to design studios?

A I have also taught seminars on modes of representation and the impact of overlapping media: these are parallel interests in my coursework. Research studios are opportunities to combine all these preoccupations in the creative act of design. I am especially interested in graduate level design research studios that have provided the forum to explore with both intensity and depth, the potential for architecture to cross the traditional disciplinary boundaries of architecture and landscape.

Q In what ways has teaching informed your professional projects?

A Teaching has had a profound impact on our professional projects. Both Michael Manfredi and I have been simultaneously teaching and practicing since we began doing competitions together as young faculty members. Teaching ensured that we had the opportunity to ask more compelling questions than those afforded by the early commissions we were able to get. We found the conceptual inquiry afforded in the academic setting offered the necessary preparation to create work that has yet to be conceived of. Without the intensity of academic inquiry, the work itself could not take on both territorial ambition and depth.

Q You titled a previous talk at Penn's 1995 "Inherited Ideologies" conference focused on the Women's Memorial project as "The Politics of Underestimation." Can you expand on this?

A It's a very interesting story. Our client for the Women's Memorial, General Wilma Vaught, was a retired General. She had a dream of creating a memorial that honored all the women who had served in the military and with her board of directors, was in search of a site to do this. One day, she was driven around the Washington, D.C. area by the director of the

---

FIGURE 1. Novartis Office Building. Photography by Paul Warchol.

FIGURE 2. Krishna P. Singh Center for Nanotechnology, University of Pennsylvania. Photography by Albert Vecerka/Esto.

A I'm really interested in the gifts that architecture can offer that allow projects—even if they're privately conceived and privately funded—to transform the public realm. The Olympic Sculpture Park in Seattle was a dream to take the often-exclusionary world of the museum and create a public setting without walls where art had room to breathe. The Barnard College Diana Center—with its luminous terracotta-colored glass diorama on Broadway—reveals the slipped volumes of the café, library, and art and architecture galleries on the façade. In our recent book *Public Natures: Evolutionary Infrastructure*, we were interested in expanding this idea to include landscape and infrastructure—identifying new terms, conditions, and models that generate productive connections between landscape, infrastructure, and urban territory—to create an architecture that is distinctly public in nature.

Q How do you think the profession should handle issues of equity and gender balance?

A Issues of equity and gender balance are evolving in mostly positive ways. Schools of architecture—including both students and faculty—are more balanced by gender than when I began teaching. Architecture, which benefits from intensity and focus, will never be easily slotted in the nine-to-five day. If support systems can evolve and grow, I think the potential for new models of leadership will continue to expand to include an even more diverse community. I am impressed by the breadth and depth of architects that are emerging—both male and female—who are simultaneously teaching, practicing, raising families, and publishing incredibly remarkable work.

Q Were there any particular influences early in your career?

A I think the first lessons came from piano. What I discovered is

National Park Service to identify potential sites. The sites were in remote and unremarkable locations and as they were returning the van, they passed by the gateway to Arlington National Cemetery—directly on axis with the Lincoln Memorial—defined by the then decrepit McKim, Meade & White retaining wall, overgrown with weeds. She asked, if she promised to renovate the wall and gateway to the cemetery, could she have permission to locate the memorial on this site. The NPS director couldn't come up with a reason to say no, and Congress ultimately approved the site selection in the shortest ever time frame recorded in Washington. No one expected her to request a more prominent site for the memorial, and no one was able to say no to an offer to rejuvenate the symbolic gateway to Arlington Cemetery.

Q Many of your academic and cultural projects focus on revealing what goes on inside. You even mentioned that architecture is a public education. What is public about architecture?

that it took an enormous amount of effort for something to finally become intuitive so that it could come out in an effortless way. That insight was one of the most useful things I discovered in architecture school. As an undergraduate, I took a figure drawing class with Carlo Pelliccia. One semester I took it for credit and continued to audit it every semester after that because it touched something I was unable to express in the studio courses. Charcoal afforded the ability to suggest rather than describe something completely and it was intuitively possible to achieve more with less. My final architecture studio was also taught by Professor Pelliccia, and while I was continuing to attempt equal success with every aspect of the assigned project, he suggested that I might benefit from focusing—just as I did with figure drawing—on the most compelling part of the brief. This has become an enduring lesson for me and we work hard to identify the essence of the question, rather than pursue the indexical compliance with every possible obligation of the project. In graduate school at Yale, I was fortunate to have design studios with both James Stirling and Andrea Leers. Jim Stirling was obviously a great hero of mine and illuminated the essential legibility of

the diagram. Andrea Leers—both a terrific architect and teacher—-insisted I abandon my inclination to drift indefinitely in search of the perfect scheme and instead pick one of them, any one of them, and bring intensity to it to make it better. In each case, I was learning the same thing in different ways—every creative endeavor requires incredible intensity, rigor, and judgement.

Q Can you expand on the ideas of layering and memory in landscapes, which are prevalent themes in your work?

A Landscape has a lot of connotations, from the picturesque to the systemic, from the territorial to the intimate. This issue of memory recognizes that landforms and landscapes have had prior lives— sometimes profoundly worth restoring. In other cases, there are narratives of disconnections that can be threaded back together in completely new ways. I'm also very interested in geological history. My mother taught cultural geography and geology, and my father was an aeronautical engineer and their shared passion for maps illuminated the value of multiple histories—often registered through landforms and

strata—that we like to unpack when we begin our research for a project. We like doing incredibly deep research before we begin a project and postpone the desire to design too quickly. This way, our intuitions can be informed by the broadest range of information, and resonances between these discoveries can guide what has the potential to become both precise and resonant.

Q Would you say that in your practice with partner Michael Manfredi, you practice differently than Michael?

A Yes, we complement each other in very different ways: we also share the same appreciation for what needs to come forward in the architecture. That's where, I would say at a certain point, both our egos have to be checked at the door because we need to nourish the DNA that's emerging in order for the ultimate design to thrive.

Q The prompt for your keynote lecture during the [RE]Form symposium centered on cultivating leadership practices and under the theme of "Converging Horizons" you presented a beautiful range of work from your professional and academic career. As both a practicing architect

FIGURE 3. Novartis Visitor Reception. Photography by Albert Vecerka/Esto.

and educator, do you find these roles easily co-exist, or do you think one influences the other more deeply? And if so, to what extent?

A I think they absolutely overlap. I've been fortunate that our practice has grown from a seed. What started out as nothing but teaching and competitions turned into something that's more robust and comprehensive. It used to be that academia was informing practice exclusively, but I would say now there's a reciprocity. Practice is also informing teaching. The incredibly complex problems that we're interested in require an enormous amount of strategic thinking to be realized in real life. I don't want students to be off the hook on that. Their ambitions are nourished directly through academic inquiry. One of the most important things about being an educator is that we need to be clear about what's at stake, how we may get there both independently and together, and why it matters.

Q At the [RE]Form symposium, it was particularly interesting when you featured two images side by side, one of Ayn Rand's Howard Roark and the other of Denise Scott Brown from *Learning from Las Vegas*. Citing Scott

FIGURE 4. Diana Center at Barnard College. Photography by Albert Vecerka/Esto.

Brown's role as an active collaborator versus Roark's depiction as a singular author, you emphasized the idea of standing on the shoulders of those who came before as well as side by side with those who are here today—both in our education and engagement. Do you feel that the future of women in architecture needs more collaboration? And if yes, what are some strategies for this to occur?

A I think they're not mutually exclusive. I think that we do stand on the shoulders of those who come before us and the view to the horizon

is so much better because of this. I met Denise Scott Brown when we were struggling to get the Women's Memorial approved by the multiple agencies in Washington, D.C. We were a year and a half into the process with little success when Denise shared a similar experience she and Bob had for the park and plaza they had designed in Washington. She was familiar with the agency roadblocks we were facing and gave me a copy of *Learning from Las Vegas*, where she inscribed the words "stand on my shoulders so you can reach for the stars." She continues to be an inspiration and embodies the long distance run that architecture truly is.

When I mentioned the collaborative act, the fact is that architects draw—they create designs. It takes a legion of people to realize it, to see it built, to fund it, to engineer it, to collaborate, to push it, to advance it. To think otherwise is profoundly arrogant. If we can learn from those who invest in it from all the different places, including our collective offices, consultants, contractors, subcontractors, and owners—if we can all keep our sights on the same horizon, but bring different strengths to the table, I think magic is possible.

Q You mentioned your interest in historic sites, studying what came before us, and what marks were left behind. How do you make sure that

FIGURE 5. Hunter's Point South Waterfront Park. Photography by Albert Vecerka/Esto.

you honor the history of both the place you design in and the people that have contributed to it?

A Sometimes history has less depth and importance than we might think—even if the forms look historically significant. The McKim, Mead & White retaining wall that had been the base of the Women's Memorial and which we transformed was from an office no longer led by McKim, Mead, or White. From our point of view, it was time to introduce a new history to honor women who had served—break through the wall, cut through those barriers, create a space, and a gallery of celebration, rather than preserve a wall that was just retaining the twenty-plus-foot grade change between the cemetery and the terminus of the memorial bridge. At the site of the Museum of the Earth, water originally traveled through the site and divided it, but this had been covered up. This inspired us to reveal the water's journey; to alter it, to have it do new things. We used the site for water retention and to reveal how engineering obligations and water purification could be part of the story of the Museum of the Earth, even if the site looked like it had no deeper history than a parking lot and existing building.

Q You mentioned that you've worked with a lot of inspiring women—who have faced many challenges. What are some of the most important lessons you've learned from them?

A We have been fortunate to have a number of inspiring women clients. Mimi Gates, the director of Seattle's Art Museum; Ruth Simmons, president of Smith's Women's College; Judith Shapiro, president of Barnard College; General Vaught, President of the Women's Memorial Foundation, and currently Kathleen Van Bergen, President of the Artis-Naples cultural campus. The list goes on, and in each case what I've learned from them is that they don't get discouraged; they share a contagious optimism and expectation that transformation is the future we all want to be a part of.

Q You noted that in architecture, you get to ask questions, find other ways of looking at things, set new passages, new horizons. What do you see on the horizon and what are you working towards?

A I see a lot of opportunities for architects to reframe and reassess the questions that are being asked. And I see the opportunity to determine what must be done and what should be done in a commission. I believe in a future where architects can assume both the role of the instigator and the designer. I look forward to the potential to have influence beyond our capacities as designers.

Q What advice would you give to young designers starting out today?

A I would say the most important thing to a designer starting today is to know that you should begin anywhere and follow your hunch about what you think is important. Then you should put all your energies and passion into seeing what that hunch can reveal. It will lead to great things—even if you don't know where you're going.

The photography featured in this article is courtesy of Weiss/Manfredi.

FIGURE 6. Seattle Art Museum: Olympic Sculpture Park. Photography by Ben Benschneider.

1

Framing Stories considers the intellectual context within which the role of women in architecture is best articulated. The larger history and theory of the discipline are brought to bear on the subject, as are new ideas for thinking about the question of gender in design. While traditional histories of the field often neglect to consider the full impact that women have had in transforming the discipline, women have more recently succeeded in framing new roles, priorities, and values for their contributions. Each of the three papers included in this section is firmly situated within existing debates on feminism. McLeod discusses its immediate history and its possible future in architecture, Berman calls for a categorical transformation in architectural education according to the principles of feminist thought, and Stratigakos reminds us to remain vigilant in our commitment to write the efforts of women architects into history—efforts constantly at risk of being lost.

framing stories

BEYOND EQUALITY

RE-GENDERING ARCHITECTURAL EDUCATION

Ila Berman

When asked what is the role that architectural education plays in the forming of women practitioners, an immediate response might simply be "to educate them—with all the means that we have available—to be successful architects." However, as not only an architect, educator, and dean, but also a feminist, I am fully aware that this response is seemingly inadequate given that it acknowledges neither the implicit and explicit forms of sexism that still exist within academia and the profession, nor the gender-biased ideological frameworks underpinning the architectural discipline in general. We have too often assumed that the issues that women are confronted with at school and the workplace are solely centered around questions of equality—that is, the equal right and opportunity for women to compete and succeed within an existing system—without questioning the biased value system that is deeply embedded within what is presented as a 'gender-neutral' education, profession, or environment.

If we, therefore, examine our current struggles against the backdrop of more than a century's efforts of women's activism, it becomes clear that, despite all that we have achieved, we are still fundamentally operating within a theoretical context reminiscent of the first wave of liberal and pragmatic feminisms of the eighteenth, nineteenth, and early twentieth centuries.[1] From this era onward, women's efforts have been primarily centered around the issue of their equality based on the argument that the only fundamental differences between men and women have been artificially and socially constructed, and that women should be granted the same educational and professional opportunities as men. The women's rights movement was thus directed toward increasing women's presence within the public realm by liberating them from gender oppression, and in many cases, overtly negating gender roles, while simultaneously transforming the institutions that historically kept women in disadvantaged positions through sex-role socialization, sexual discrimination, lack of access to education and job training, unequal wages, and lack of recognition and advancement within the workplace, among other tactics. Progress on this front has been accomplished by ensuring that our social and political institutions and their structures are vigilant in warranting equal access to education, legal rights, and professional advancement not only by intensifying awareness of these issues, but more importantly through legal instruments, policy, and direct action.

These efforts have occupied the majority of the women's movement as a whole and, over the last three decades, have been responsible for the rapidly increasing population of women in universities, and, more specifically, within architectural programs throughout North America. Many American universities were either segregated or denied women access until as late as the 1960s and 1970s when the Supreme Court's backing of civil rights legislation threatened to eliminate the prejudices against women that had kept them out of institutions of higher education. Thus, despite its 200-year history, the University of Virginia (UVA) (where I am currently dean of the Architecture School)—touted as the oldest public university in the United States—only first fully admitted women in 1971. For more than 150 of these 200 years, therefore, UVA was exclusively for men. It remains important that this institution emerged as a public university that was both secular and accessible to all. Cementing the legacy of Thomas Jefferson, it made possible an enlightened and educated democracy.[2] And yet, for the vast majority of its history, this institution excluded women who were not considered part of what constituted the so-called public. Women were deprived not only of the right to be educated and the right to a profession, but also of the more basic human right to exist within the public sphere. In being relegated to the realm of the invisible, women were therefore marginalized within humanity itself.

> The human norm stands for normality, normalcy, and normativity. It functions by transposing a specific mode of being human into a generalized standard, which acquires transcendent values as the human: from male to masculine and onto human as the universalized format of humanity. This standard is posited as categorically and qualitatively distinct from the sexualized, racialized, naturalized others.[3]

Continually reminding ourselves and others of these obvious yet hidden facts—by exposing the highly gendered specificity behind histories that present themselves as normative and neutral—is part of what it means to be a feminist.

In 1972, the U.S. Department of Education's Office of Civil rights enforced Title IX of the educational amendments in order to protect people, in educational programs that receive federal assistance, from discrimination based on sex.[4] This legislation changed the course of history for women. Despite limitations on this legislation to institutions and programs receiving public funds, and the very short time frame within which women gained access to higher education, by the mid-1980s, and in every year since, more undergraduate and graduate degrees have been conferred on women than men in the United States—proving the earlier assertions of the women's movement that women would excel in institutions of higher learning once given equal opportunity.[5]

Traditionally masculinized professions such as architecture, however, have taken longer to reach equal numbers of both female applicants and admitted students. In 2016 the National Architectural Accrediting Board (NAAB) indicated in its annual report that forty-six percent (11,223) of a total of 24,456 enrolled students in accredited architecture programs were female, and forty-three percent of a total of 6,042 architecture degrees were awarded to women.[6] Thus, it is only in recent years that schools of architecture in this country, those that were once the bastions of white males, are now approaching equal numbers of women. Four and a half decades after the early legislation against sex discrimination in education was passed, we now live in different times: women are not only seeing architecture as a viable profession and career path, but also often excel beyond their male counterparts in an admissions process that purports to be gender-blind, such that the number of female architecture students and female architecture graduates is steadily climbing. Our work, however, continues, albeit perhaps in a different vein. This includes not only protecting Title IX legislation that has come under siege by misogynist protagonists within our current political climate,[7] but also ensuring that we continue to examine the gendered ideologies that are still entrenched within architectural academia.

Female students require female mentors to succeed, just as female faculty depend upon support at senior administrative levels for their advancement. The comparative percentages of female professors of architecture have obviously trailed behind those of female architecture students, while also decreasing as one moves toward leadership roles. This is in part because it has taken years to produce a comparable percentage of women competing for architectural positions within schools of architecture, but more importantly because of the slow rate of turnover within academia and the gender biases that occur not only within hiring procedures, but also throughout the processes responsible for inviting visitors—faculty, lecturers, and symposium participants—to the university. In 2015-16, thirty-one percent (872) of full- and part-time ranked faculty in architecture were women, an increase of two percent from the previous year.[8] Of these, the majority (forty percent) were assistant professors since only twenty-three percent—less than a quarter—of full professors in architecture, at this time, were women. Given the context of tenure and lifetime appointments in education, evolution in the full-time faculty of architecture schools is slow; unless there is growth, positions open only when individuals retire, and competition for these positions is extremely high.

We also operate in a field where peer-review dominates the hiring process, promotion, tenure, awards, and recognitions. As was made clear in the data presented in 2014 by Lian Chang, the past director of Research + Information of the Association of Collegiate Schools of Architecture (ACSA), the percentage of women in architecture radically decreases as one moves up the pipeline toward more senior positions and higher level awards, honors, and recognitions such as deanships, distinguished professor awards, and medals for teaching and professional practice.[9] Medals and high level honors and positions for women require strong advocates just as equitable peer-review processes demand equal gender representation among those conducting such reviews. Equal representation, however, seldom occurs and even when it does, it doesn't guarantee a true cultural shift given the propensity for internalized sexism among women who have succeeded within patriarchal systems and the need for conceptual tools to help us recognize and confront this. The requirement for advocacy is critical. Historically, the disenfranchisement of women at the upper levels of academia has had as much to do with women's persistent invisibility within male-centric systems as with the cloning mechanisms implicitly operating through such practices of advancement; where men are both hired and mentored more predominantly than women—a practice that is mirrored within the profession. In my position as dean, acting as an advocate and mentor for female architects, faculty, and students is, therefore, one of my most important roles.

Efforts toward equity within architecture and, more importantly, the elimination of hidden forms of gender-bias, are absolutely necessary and vital, yet these actions still represent but a moderate position in relation to the true emancipation of women, primarily because the framework upon which these actions depend remains uncritically assimilationist.

Models of equality are, at most, a superficial critique of culture because they do not question the underlying ideologies that form and structure our social values and the pervasive complicity of values considered to be normative with patriarchy. These ideologies support and maintain what Russell Ferguson has referred to as the 'invisible center' or 'mythical norm'—the white, young, heterosexual, Christian, financially secure male—the place from which power is exerted, and that defines the standard against which all sexualized and racialized 'others' are measured, since man stands for, and has become, the universal signifier for humanity in general.[10] This is of course why when we see rooms, review panels, boards, or symposia populated almost entirely by men, time and time again, no one seems to notice (and we certainly don't imagine that the focus of these gatherings is on men's issues even if that might implicitly be the case). Yet, if we see those same rooms, panels, boards, and symposia populated by women, we automatically assume that they are dealing with issues specifically related to women. That women's rights are not intrinsically considered to be human rights, but rather a sub-category of rights supporting a special interest group, is because humanity, akin to our notions of the 'public,' has historically been gendered as male. Hillary Clinton's dictum: "Women's rights are human rights," and human rights are women's rights is a critical statement that calls attention to how we might rethink and address this issue.[11]

In order to problematize the question of equality for women, psychoanalyst and theorist Luce Irigaray has written:

> Demanding equality as women is, it seems to me, a mistaken expression of a real objective. The demand to be equal presupposes a point of comparison. To whom or to what do women want to be equalized? To men? To a salary? To a public office? To what standard? Why not to themselves?[12]

Irigaray's critique demands an investigation of the ideological underpinnings of the equal rights movement, in order to more radically redefine the issues facing women. She rejects the presupposition that as women we should continue to be defined in relation to the very structures responsible for our disenfranchisement. Rather, women should reposition themselves at the center, instead of at the margins, and ask the larger question: "what is it that women want?" In her essay: "Equal or Different," she further posits that since the exploitation of women is based upon sexual difference, it can therefore only be resolved through sexual difference. Her critique of the wholesale neutralization of sex, or the reduction of true biological difference to socially constructed difference—what we define as gender, is based on the fact that the human species is divided into two sexes to ensure its production and reproduction.[13] To suppress this condition is to not only negate the very specific and violent history that led women to be branded as "less than human others" in relation to a masculinized self-serving humanism constructed by, and for men, but also, in a more positive vein, to suppress

the distinct values that might emerge from this difference—values to which women might subscribe and that would radically question the highly gendered anthropocentric norms to which we have assimilated.

Although earlier socialist feminisms critiqued the generative structures of power and the ahistoricity of gender politics, they were still criticized by radical Anglo-American feminists and theoretical French feminists alike for privileging masculinist values—the public, social, political, and economic spheres—while diminishing those that had historically been gendered as feminine—the private, bodily, psychic, and aesthetic. Further, feminist advocates of 'difference' claimed that it is not simply that real women are oppressed within educational, legal, and economic structures, but also that this oppression is implicated by the way in which the feminine has been simultaneously repressed in language, philosophy, and culture. Theorists of sexual difference, therefore, advanced a feminism that would not only be critical of the patriarchy that it de-territorializes, but it would also be situated, that is, concretely embodied, and creatively affirmative in producing a new agenda. They thus stress the necessity for women to write, speak, design, and construct their own material and conceptual futures. Irigaray is certainly not advocating that sexuality wholly define our professional lives but rather that we recognize differences that are critical to our reformulation of cultural, educational, and professional values as women including "issues associated with the respect for life and culture, and with the continuous passage of the natural into the cultural."[14] She continues:

> One of the main obstacles to the creation and recognition of such values is the more or less obscure hold patriarchal and phallocratic models have had for centuries over the whole of our civilization. It is quite simply a matter of social justice to balance out this power of the one sex over the other by giving, or giving back, cultural values to female sexuality.[15]

Following the second wave of feminism—the civil rights movement and the radical feminisms of the 1960s and 1970s whose work was directed toward liberating women from subjugation and male supremacist oppression[16]—theories of sexual difference led by women such as Luce Irigaray and Hélène Cixous in the third wave of feminism,[17] interrogated assumptions about equality. They questioned the requisite assimilation of women to male normative standards while scrutinizing the supposed neutrality of values at their core.[18] The implicit gender-bias hidden behind the structure of this universal norm was thus exposed, by making conspicuous the relations between its power, its ubiquity, and its surreptitiousness, and by foregrounding the correspondence between the construction of the universal subject and the self-serving prototype of the white, Christian, heterosexual male. As Ferguson so correctly notes: "while the myth is perpetuated by those whose interests it serves, it can also be internalized by those who are oppressed by it."[19] Being a woman therefore does not automatically make you a feminist, nor does it mean that you will advocate on behalf of women since our struggles as female architects and educators are implicated by the biases that we have all internalized and the mythical norms to which we have so readily assimilated. For women, as for any marginalized group, assimilation to these norms can only be exacted at a price: a massive repression which demands that one erase one's own biology, history, ethnicity, sexuality, values, and experiences and replace them with those of the dominant group—the prevailing, and in this case phallogocentric, ideology. This assimilation occurs through the process of socialization and is responsible for what Cornel West refers to as double-consciousness—where we, by the nature of our own highly gendered education, have been systematically trained to not only interiorize our own marginality, but also identify against ourselves.[20] So for those of us that may have succeeded within a male dominated system, we feel that we are both a part of this system and yet still in some ways separated from, or marginalized by it.

In order to transform our environment, we must first exorcise the essential white male subject implanted within each of us.

And what better example of the extent of women's double-consciousness and internalized misogyny and racism than what we witnessed during the most recent election in this country where close to fifty percent of women voted for an abusive and bullying misogynist, and one third of Hispanics and Asians voted for a racist. It seems that only our millennial youth, who care enough about the future since it is their future and do not want to have it destroyed, and African American women, consistently voted with their own identities, subjectivities, and self-interests intact. In the latter case, it would seem that the overlay of race and gender—a form of intensified double marginalization—provided the needed inoculation to the schizophrenia of double-consciousness, since these women are neither privileged by being male or white. As Jonathan Culler has written:

the most insidious form of oppression alienates a group from its own interests as a group and encourages it to identify with the interests of its oppressors, so that political struggles must first awaken a group to its interests and its experience.[21]

This awakening, or raising consciousness, operates as a form of re-centering that not only acts to critique the assimilationist model, but also provides an affirmative lens through which to create alternative subjectivities and new frameworks for our discipline.

Our highly individualistic, self-centered, consumption and competition-driven culture cannot therefore be dissociated from the highly gendered place from which it originated (encouraged, no doubt, by testosterone infused bodies that consistently celebrate the one over the many while leaving the debris of territorial skirmishes in their wakes); just as women's equality within architecture cannot be pursued without simultaneously interrogating and exposing the invisible and highly gendered frameworks and power structures that define both the discipline and profession. This critique is a necessary prelude to a more affirmative model that would allow us to imagine both the re-gendering of our educational models towards integrating feminist perspectives into the classroom, and the re-gendering of the architectural profession itself. We have to, therefore, ask ourselves: what are the values to which we have subscribed within architectural education and practice? Are they our own? And if not, what can we do to transform them?

Through this re-gendering of architectural education, we might imagine a number of phenomena. First, and foremost, as feminists it is crucial that we replace the archaic image of the heroic white male master-designer-builder with a broader and collaborative framework for design, which is more inclusive in both its practice and modes of recognition, and imagines a wider range of professional opportunities to which our education leads. The emphasis on individual autonomy and individual success (with all of its narcissistic 'delusions of grandeur') is a highly gendered phenomenon. According to feminist scholar Rosi Braidotti, the phallocratic:

> humanistic ideal constituted, in fact, the core of a liberal individualistic view of the subject, which defined perfectibility in terms of autonomy and self-determination … Individualism is not an intrinsic part of 'human nature,' as liberal thinkers are prone to believe, but rather a historically and culturally specific discursive formation, one which, moreover, is becoming increasingly problematic.[22]

In some corners of the profession, this overt emphasis on individual autonomy and overly hierarchical structures of practice are already being replaced by complex constellations that bring together and synthesize multiple forms of expertise to generate architectural products that are shared rather than being captured and territorialized under a single author/owner. Within existing models of architectural authorship, creative forms of work are often rendered invisible under those (predominantly men) that are seen to lead these 'signature' architectural practices. Not until this work, and those that have generated it, are publicly acknowledged as meaningfully contributing to the success of those practices (rather than being subsumed as feminized and "mute" material labor) will architecture evolve into a more equitable profession.

As an alternative to this hierarchical model led by the 'heroic' architect, feminism should offer a more relational model of subjectivity able to mobilize empathy and mediate differences across a wide-ranging and complex set of needs and desires. We might therefore teach students to more effectively collaborate as an integral part of their education, since outside of school, no one ever practices architecture alone.

The ability to communicate productively, share knowledge and experience, and work well with others is critical to success in practice, yet seldom is this taught within architecture schools in an intentional way.

Second, in re-gendering architectural education, we should also be asking how might we move away from the typical competitive model of education and practice, toward a more collaborative, iterative, and inclusive model that collectively advances architectural excellence rather than exceptionalism, and that supports differently defined qualitative cultural values across scales, practices, domains, and territories. Excellence within this context would be a shared common goal, attained through collective products that are greater than what a single individual, firm or institution could provide, and whose value might be immanent to the material and living energy invested in their making and gleaned from their experience rather than solely determined by comparison to an external standard, metric, or norm. Only when immanent material value is able to withstand being transcoded into abstract exchange value, will architecture and design—the handmaidens of capitalism—be able

to resist their wholesale commodification. This is especially critical at a time where the exchange value of space and property outstrips (or remains entirely disconnected from) the immanent value of the architectural works being exchanged.

Third, it is important that we recognize the diversification of opportunities both within and outside of the profession of architecture for which we are educating students, and the space needed for this within our curricula. It is clear that architecture has seen tremendous growth and development in practice over the last twenty years and the products of those practices are continuously evolving. Architectural education has similarly become increasingly diversified internally, as specializations across a wide range of disciplinary domains—from ecology to technology—have substantially changed the academic environment. What had at one time occupied the margins of the discipline have thus come to occupy its center: all of this, occurring in parallel with the increasing number and percentage of women in the discipline. This complexification of the discipline, as it stretches into fields related to, or implicated by its practice, operates as a resistance to the idea of architectural essentialism—that there is a key set of objects, models, methods, truths, and areas of knowledge that define the center of the architectural canon. Should we be surprised then, that at the same moment when we witness a backlash against women on the stage of politics and within society, we see a concurrent retrenchment of architecture within academia and a call to return to its historically delimited boundaries?[23] Rather than a return, perhaps we should be questioning why architecture had originally moved beyond its earlier limitations in the first place, and ask how this disciplinary expansion might contribute to the positive evolution and reshaping of professional practice. The path to licensure is obviously not the only standard to which we should be subscribing, and perhaps, as part of the discussion of the missing thirty-two percent within practice,[24] we need to diversify the structure of both practice and licensure itself.

This expansive and relational model of architectural education might also lead to more intense affiliations with other associated disciplinary practices especially those that had been historically subjugated by the built environment. We have already seen a rise in prominence of landscape practices within architecture, at the very moment that the environment—another highly gendered territory—is foregrounded and given a voice. Landscape architecture's lead in defining new ecological and environmental models that have enabled us to rethink architecture and urbanism in terms of their metabolic, material, and performative processes has been transformative for the profession and education, and also for our expanding models of subjectivity. As stated by Braidotti, a "powerful source of inspiration for contemporary reconfigurations of critical post-humanism is ecology and environmentalism. They rest on an enlarged sense of inter-connection between self and others, including the non-human or 'earth' others."[25] Understanding that the larger biosphere is a support for all forms of life, human and non-human, is critical for our collective future. And yet, as the Environmental Protection Agency (EPA) is being systematically dismantled in the United States, hard won battles to secure environmental protections meant to ensure the survival of life on this planet are continuously being threatened; something we should recognize as both a feminist and ecological issue, since the raping and instrumentalization of the environment (another vital and material 'other') and the exploitation of women, have historically gone hand in hand.

Affiliations with practices such as landscape architecture, urban design, and other fields, strengthen the interconnectivity of architecture with its sister disciplines, and contribute to its participatory value in the design and emergence of more integrated large-scale territories. As we extend this relational model, it might also lead to the development of stronger interdisciplinary collaborative structures that move outside of the narrow band of our related disciplines in order to address larger issues and have a greater collective positive impact on populations, environments, and communities underserved by architecture.

Just as human rights are women's rights, social justice issues are equally feminist issues, asking us to question who has traditionally benefited, and alternatively who should benefit from architectural and urban expertise.

Why is design that is in service to the public good not located at the core of our practices? Consistent with the revolutionary legacy at UVA, our mission as a school of architecture is to produce the next generation of innovative leaders, thinkers, designers, and makers who will not only engage the most difficult challenges of our time, but also envision, design, and build the most just, compelling, and courageous of futures. This mission, certainly, cannot be achieved when disciplines operate in distinct silos across which there are few channels for communication.

Through our Next Cities Institute at UVA, for example, we are focused on the most pressing global challenges: planetary urbanization and migration, climate change and environmental degradation, social justice issues, and the accelerating transformation of information technologies that are fundamentally reshaping our cities and environments. Here, we are working on projects in the Arctic, Asia, and across the Global South in urban Africa, Latin America, and India—vast territories often covered by invisible cities and informal settlements within which urban transformation is occurring at an unprecedented rate. These territories constitute a massive form of 'feminine' planetary matter often hidden or overlooked, understood as existing beyond or outside of the purview of professional architectural interests. Through efforts such as the Yamuna River project in Delhi, India, we are using design methodologies to address extremely difficult urban, architectural, and environmental problems while working with other disciplines such as engineering, environmental science, politics, and public health to set up collaborative models for integrated research.

Lastly, within the larger context of advanced educational institutions, it is important that we are re-positioning design at the center, rather than the periphery of research. This needs to happen both through the development of design-based research methodologies within architecture, and by exporting design education—its synthetic methodologies, approaches to experiential learning, and focus on creative making, problem-solving, and experimentation—to other disciplines. Nurturing the vital and creative impulse is intrinsic to design education, yet it is undervalued in institutions that determine academic value, to a large extent, because they favor quantitative research metrics determined solely by journal paper citations, paper productivity, and federally funded grants. In recent years, schools of architecture have uncritically absorbed this definition of research with its implicitly held definitions of value without questioning the biases (rooted in the dogma of scientific reason) operating at its core, just as equality-minded feminists donned the uniforms and suits of their male counterparts without interrogating the hidden anthropocentric and masculinist subjectivities intrinsic to the norms to which they were subscribing. Within academia, where research and rationality are deemed more important than creativity, and metrics trump poetics, architecture schools will always operate at a disadvantage given that they are being pressured to assimilate to a value structure that ensures in advance, the subjugation and devaluation of their core practices. How does one quantify the number of times a work of architecture is viewed and experienced and the impact that this might have on a life, a population, or the next generation of cultural makers? What is the equivalent of a citation in architectural practice where the use of critical architectural precedents and the liberal borrowing of visual tropes is typical yet remains undocumented in any precise way? Why is the writing about architecture through peer-reviewed paper presentations, journal articles, and books more significant, from a research perspective, than drawings and images (and other visual methods of elucidating projects) that more closely align with their reality and that are a critical part of their theorization and representation? These are questions that attempt to acknowledge the ways in which architecture has already been cast as a 'feminine' discipline within the academy, its recent attempts to be taken more seriously by adopting masculinist metricized research paradigms, and potential modes of resistance to, and/or creative transformations of such paradigms.

As we advance within architectural education, it is imperative that we move away from an overly simplified binary model that casts women in one of two roles, neither of which they have historically authored. Rather, we might escape this dualism and move toward "a transformative or symbiotic relation that hybridizes and alters the 'nature' of each one [while foregrounding] the middle grounds of their interaction."[26] We should acknowledge that women will assuredly succeed in traditionally masculinized subdisciplines within architecture, such as advanced computational and building technologies, without assuming that the feminist extension of women into these fields implies the wholesale adoption of the technological and scientific imperialist paradigm from which these evolved. As a potential space of critique, transformation, and affirmation, these women might instead inhabit these disciplines in order to reinvent their practices while simultaneously redirecting them (following the legacy of Haraway and Braidotti) to support, rather than dominate, the living. Feminist practices within architectural education, therefore, ironically necessitate a 'double-edged vision' that intermixes and negotiates between dominant norms and alternative forms of practice. This enables a nondialectical and nonunitary feminist subjectivity "that works across differences and is also internally differentiated, but still grounded and accountable"[27] within a larger interdependent collectivity.

The transformation within schools of architecture is certainly evident in both the quantity of female students and the diversity and extraordinary quality of their work. Their work follows no simplistic gendered categorization, perhaps for the very reason that their evolution has already exceeded the conceptual framing of post-structural feminisms of the 1990s. This has enabled them to focus on, and collectively write their own conceptual and material futures rather than inadvertently assimilate to male normative behaviors or be mired in architectural histories focused on the exclusion and subjugation of women. While the project of continuously mining, theorizing, and writing this absent or unseen history is absolutely critical and necessary to deepen our collective memory, it is perhaps not the place from which this generation of female students and architects will find their voice. What is more important are the ways in which architectural education and practice, as vital matters in their own right, are being re-gendered due to the very real transformation of the population within it.

The necessity to write one's own history as women, as stated by Hélène Cixous, is the only way forward, even as it demands that we interrogate and continually challenge the assumptions we've inherited.

This points to specific opportunities for architectural education and practice, by scrutinizing the theoretical frameworks operating within the discipline, while strategically applying those that have emerged from feminist discourses onto the very structures through which we are educating students. This of course, needs to happen concurrent with concrete initiatives that ensure there are visible women leaders and role models at all levels of education and practice, and that they are being recognized for their ongoing work. Perhaps through this process we will not only educate an entirely different type of female architectural practitioner, but might also dissolve the gap that currently exists between education and practice, so that the re-gendering of education and its transformation ultimately contribute, over time, to the creative re-gendering of practice.

Endnotes

1   Although the genealogy of feminism is complex, the first wave of liberal feminism is considered to have emerged in the mid- to late-eighteenth century and continued through the nineteenth century in the agendas of Mary Wollstonecraft (1759-1797), Frances Wright (1795-1852), Sarah Grimke (1792-1873), Sojourner Truth (1795-1883), Elizabeth Cady Stanton (1815-1902), Susan B. Anthony (1820-1906), Harriet Taylor (1807-1858), and John Stuart Mill (1806-1873). Enlightenment liberal feminists shared the following basic tenets: [1] Faith in rationality (in accordance with enlightenment belief); [2] Belief that women's and men's souls and rational faculties are the same; [3] Belief in education as the means to institute social change and transform society; [4] Autonomy: view of the Individual as an isolated, independent agent whose dignity depends on such independence; [5] Belief in the doctrine of natural rights.

2   "I know no safe depositary of the ultimate powers of the society but the people themselves; and if we think them not enlightened enough to exercise their control with a wholesome discretion, the remedy is not to take it from them, but to inform their discretion by education. This is the true corrective of abuses of constitutional power." Thomas Jefferson to William C. Jarvis, Monticello, September 28, 1820.
"Convinced that the people are the only safe depositories of their own liberty, and that they are not safe unless enlightened to a certain degree, I have looked on our present state of liberty as a short-lived possession unless the mass of the people could be informed to a certain degree." Thomas Jefferson to Littleton Waller Tazewell, January 5, 1805.

3   Rosi Braidotti, *The Posthuman* (Cambridge, UK: Polity Press, 2013), 26.

4   Kristen M. Galles, "Filling the Gaps: Women, Civil Rights and Title IX," American Bar Association, June 30, 2017, https://www.americanbar.org/groups/crsj/publications/human_rights_magazine_home/human.

5   National Center for Education Statistics, *Digest of Education Statistics*, accessed September 12, 2017, https://nces.ed.gov/programs/digest/.

6   *NAAB 2016 Annual Report Part I*, 11, http://www.naab.org/accreditation/publications/.

7   On September 7, 2017, Betsy DeVos announced plans to roll back federal guidance on Title IX threatening civil rights protections for students. See Stephanie Saul and Kate Taylor, "Betsy DeVos Reverses Obama-era Policy on Campus Sexual Assault Investigations," *The New York Times*, September 22, 2017, https://www.nytimes.com/2017/09/22/us/devos-colleges-sex-assault.html.

8   *NAAB 2016 Annual Report Part II*, 2, http://www.naab.org/accreditation/publications/.

9   Lian Chikako Chang, "Where Are the Women? Measuring Progress on Gender in Architecture," October 2014, accessed March 18, 2019, http://www.acsa-arch.org/resources/data-resources/women.

10 Russell Ferguson, "Introduction: Invisible Center," in *Out There: Marginalization and Contemporary Culture*, ed. Russell Ferguson, Martha Gever, Trinh T. Minh-ha, and Cornel West (Cambridge: MIT Press, 1990), 9.

11 This was the title of a speech by Hillary Rodham Clinton, the then first lady of the United States, given at the UN Fourth World Conference on Women in Beijing on September 5, 1995. It was considered to be drawn from the phrasing of the early feminists Sarah Moore Grimké and Angelina Grimké Weld in the 1830s in a series of Letters on the Equality of the Sexes. See Catherine H. Birney, *The Grimke Sisters, Sarah and Angelina Grimke: the First American Women Advocates of Abolition and Women's Rights* (Boston: Lee and Shepard,1885), 109.

12 Luce Irigaray, "Women Equal or Different," in *je, tu, nous: Toward a Culture of Difference*, trans. Alison Martin. (New York: Routledge, 1993), 12.

13 Ibid.

14 Ibid., 13.

15 Ibid., 12-13.

16 The civil rights and feminist movements of the 1960s and seventies are considered to be those that constitute the second-wave of the feminist movement, which built upon not only the first-wave of liberal and pragmatic feminists, but also feminist themes that continued throughout modernism such as Marxist and socialist feminism. Although Marxist and socialist feminists have much in common, they are separated by one major difference: whereas socialist feminists believe that gender and class play an approximately equal role in any explanation of women's oppression, Marxist feminists believe that class ultimately better accounts for women's status and function. Critical of assimilationism, Marxist and socialist feminists believe that the structure of women's oppression is entirely rooted in the existing political, social, and economic structures and that equality can only be enacted through their basic restructuring.

17 Third-wave feminism, which emerged in the 1990s, was constructed around theories of 'difference' imported primarily through French theorists such as Luce Irigaray, Hélène Cixous, Julia Kristeva, and others. It built on, yet distinguished itself from late modern radical feminist theory the latter of which claimed that male supremacy and the subjugation of women is the root and model oppression in society, that colonialization is inherently patriarchal, and that feminism has to be the basis for any truly revolutionary change. Radical feminism recognizes and affirms that women and men are fundamentally different. It attempts to resist and subvert male-dominance by displacing the phallocentricity of present culture through consciousness raising and the creation of practices and work that specifically express the subjectivity of women. While it positions itself as a critique of dominant patriarchal institutions, its main interest is to counter the forces, both ideological and violent, responsible for women's oppression. On the one hand, it counters misogynist practices that form the basis for patriarchal rule such as sexual violence against women, while on the other hand, it critiques and transforms the anxiety and alienation-producing conditions that subjugate women who blindly subscribe to assimilationist models. One of the largest differences between the work of the French feminists and Anglo-American feminists is that while the former focused on the theoretical problematization of gender within a philosophico-linguistic and psychoanalytic tradition, the latter had a more sociological and pragmatic emphasis. It attempts to exorcise the white male heterosexist subject implanted within all women by focusing on the affirmative force of female expression and its capacity to generate a gynocentric symbol.

18 Continental feminisms within this third wave problematized the profoundly humanist Anglo-American subject which had regarded woman as an essential self that needs to be liberated from oppressive social relations. Although the radical feminism of the '70s, by reversing masculine/feminine value systems, countered the re-inscription of patriarchy by rejecting assimilationist practices, it did not submit to scrutiny the patriarchal epistemological foundation of the binary oppositional structures that it often left intact. Notwithstanding the fact that there are many similarities between radical feminists and the theorists of 'difference,' French feminists such as Hélène Cixous and Luce Irigaray extended both the critique and affirmative stance of radical feminists by challenging and unsettling the coherence of those oppositional structures subsumed under the royal binary pair: man/woman. The subversion of the binary couple allowed women to move outside of the realm of opposition and complementarity, by revealing the ways in which woman, the feminine and female sexuality necessarily exceed the roles they have been assigned within this structure. Irigaray and Cixous re-instate the female body and the feminine treating both as sites for exploration in feminist politics. Otherness or alterity is here linked positively to the issue of sexual difference in order to advance a 'feminism' that is concretely embodied ('situated'), critical (of the patriarchy it deterritorializes), and yet creatively affirmative in its becoming.

19 Ferguson, "Introduction," 9.

20 Cornel West, "The New Cultural Politics of Difference," in *Out There: Marginalization and Contemporary Culture*, ed. Russell Ferguson, Martha Gever, Trinh T. Minh-ha, and Cornel West (Cambridge: MIT Press, 1990), 28.

21 Johnathan Culler, *On Deconstruction: Theory and Criticism after Structuralism* (Ithaca, NY: Cornell University Press, 1982), 50.

22 Braidotti, *The Posthuman,* 23.

23 I am referring here to the post-digital (and post-ecological and post-urban) tendencies of many current schools of architecture to return to a 'building-focused' curriculum, the reconsideration of historical typologies, and an emphasis on drawing and representation techniques reminiscent of the post-modern, neo-historicism of the early 1980s. Rem Koolhaas's Venice Architectural Biennale, focused on the "Elements of Architecture," was a clear indicator of this shift away from the diverse territories of earlier biennales, and a return to previously defined architectural fundamentals as a re-inscription of its longstanding (and highly masculinized) identity.

24 See Equity by Design survey conducted in collaboration with the American Institute of Architects (AIA) regarding the 'missing 32% campaign' that was started in California. This refers to the gap between the percentage of female students being educated (approaching 50%) and those that have been licensed as architects (18%). See *EQxD - Equity in Architecture Survey Final Report 2014*. San Francisco, CA: Equity by Design Committee and AIA San Francisco, 2015, https://issuu.com/rsheng2/docs/equityinarch2014_finalreport.

25 Braidotti, *The Posthuman,* 47.

26 Ibid.,79.

27 Ibid., 49.

THE RISE AND FALL

AND RISE AGAIN (?) OF FEMINIST ARCHITECTURE HISTORY

Mary McLeod

Today, on both sides of the Atlantic, there is a renewed interest among students, women architects, and architecture historians in gender and feminist thought.

Despite the increasing numbers of women students, persistent inequalities in professional registration and office status have motivated a new generation of women architects to engage once again in efforts to combat blatant and more subtle forms of discrimination. They are forming activist groups, organizing conferences and events devoted to women's issues, and campaigning to change professional organizations and how offices are structured.

However, even with this renewed activism, a rich and diverse legacy of earlier feminist architecture history seems to have been nearly forgotten. When I talked to a group of students at a meeting of ArchiteXX held in April 2014 at Columbia University and asked them who they considered to be the first feminist architecture historians, no one could name even a single individual who had published before the mid-1980s. More recently, I have had the same response at other architecture schools in both Europe and the United States.

So it is in that spirit that I present this brief account of the evolution of the major currents in American feminist architecture history from the early 1970s to 2000, and then offer some personal reflections on issues that I believe deserve further consideration.

This evolution can be seen as falling into three phases, reflecting in part the evolution of Anglo-American feminist thinking itself. The first phase was closely tied with the intense change in consciousness that struck the United States in the late 1960s. Evolving directly out of the civil-rights and anti-war movements, and spurred by American and British books such as Betty Friedan's *The Feminist Mystique* (1963), Kate Millet's *Sexual Politics* (1970), and Juliet Mitchell's *Woman's Estate* (1971), the feminist movement quickly became a major political and cultural force, one that pressed for reproductive rights, equal pay, child care, and radical change in the construction of gender roles. The impact on the architecture profession in the United States was almost immediate. By the mid-1970s, the number of women in university architecture programs went from just a token of one or two to being nearly a third of all students; by the late 1970s, a flood of these young graduates began to enter practice.[1]

Contemporaneously, women architects and scholars, often outside or at the margins of academia, began to rethink the history of modern architecture. They were motivated by two major objectives: to recognize women designers who had been forgotten or undervalued in the history of modern architecture, and to reconsider the nature and boundaries of the profession in order to embrace more fully women's experience, most notably in the domestic realm.

Both goals characterize two fundamental works of this first period: Susana Torre's exhibition *Women in American Architecture: A Historic and Contemporary Perspective*, sponsored by the Architectural League of New York in 1977 and Dolores Hayden's book *The Grand Domestic Revolution: A History of Feminist Designs for American Homes, Neighborhoods, and Cities* in 1981.

Torre's modestly titled exhibition had a revolutionary impact, bringing to prominence a myriad of talented and innovative designers who had been overlooked in both the historical and contemporary press: Julia Morgan, Eleanor Raymond, Marion Mahony Griffin, Natalie de Blois, Anne Griswold Tyng, and Denise Scott Brown, among others. This diverse and eclectic grouping challenged the very notion of a historical canon and the standard lineage of heroic male architects. In addition, the show revealed a dimension of American architecture history that had been previously ignored: the intersection of an earlier women's movement in the United States with a vigorous campaign for domestic reform that extended from the 1860s to the 1930s, a subject explored in three essays in the exhibition catalog by Dolores Hayden and Gwendolyn Wright.

Four years later, Hayden's ground-breaking study, *The Grand Domestic Revolution*, expanded on this research. Instead of discussing masterpieces or canonical figures, the book examined a series of experimental efforts to restructure living arrangements; these early feminist proposals not only anticipated many of the innovations of the Modern Movement but also underscored the need for contemporary transformations in the domestic realm. Wright's book *Moralism and Model Home*, though more circumscribed in scope (focusing on Chicago in the first decades of the twentieth century), investigated similar territory. In both books, style was not the issue: what mattered was the connection between the physical environment and the way we live. And once again, numerous women who had been omitted from traditional architecture surveys came to the fore: Catharine

Beecher, Melusina Fay Peirce, Charlotte Perkins Gilman, Alice Constance Austin, and Christine Frederick. Even more important, Hayden's and Wright's new feminist histories questioned the very parameters of architecture itself. Whereas the Modern Movement had extended the conception of architecture to worker's housing, they reversed the equation: housing, whether designed by architects or not, must be part of architecture—and its history. A more comprehensive understanding of the intersections of material and domestic culture, they argued, was fundamental to any reformation of architecture itself.

This same fervent commitment to social change marked the special issue of the feminist art journal *Heresies*, published in 1981, *Making Room: Women and Architecture*. The process of creation—collaborative, democratic, and consensual (which also meant long, drawn-out meetings, involving endless negotiations)—was to its participants as important as its final contents. The boldness and diversity of this phase of feminism is fully apparent in this collective endeavor; and the groundwork for many subsequent studies can be found here, despite the naïveté and utopianism of some of the more revolutionary claims. The special issue included Leslie Weisman's manifesto "A Women's Environmental Rights," proclamations of a 'feminist' aesthetic, and essays on topics as varied as urban social issues, vernacular environments, women landscape architects, European modernists (Lilly Reich and Eileen Gray), and gender divisions in non-'Western' spaces. Historical writings were interspersed with reports on alternative design practices and projects for birth centers, housing, and even a memorial dance hall, dedicated to blues singer Bessie Smith. In its optimism and activism, *Making Room* was similar to several other experimental endeavors of this era, including the Feminist Art Program's exhibition *Womanhouse* (1971–72), the Woman's Building in Los Angeles (1973–91)**,** and the Women's School of Planning and Architecture, founded by in 1974.

By the early 1980s, this activist commitment to social transformation had touched even such traditional institutions as Columbia University's Graduate School of Architecture, Planning, and Preservation (GSAPP), and the Society of Architectural Historians (SAH); in 1982–83, Columbia's architecture program sponsored a lecture series on feminist perspectives on the built environment, and in 1985, Elizabeth Grossman organized the first SAH session on women in architecture. For a generation of women architects, these events and publications shook the East Coast architecture establishment's faith in the importance of abstract formal explorations—whether the arcane Corbusian explorations of the New York Five or the mannerist inversions of historicist post-modernists. In architecture history, it brought a greater attention to marginal tendencies and figures, a new interest in material and social history, and a vision of scholarship as actively engaged in present-day transformations.

A few years later, however, feminist thinking in architecture began to take a radically different direction—less activist, and more theoretical, i.e., more focused on representation than practice. The objective was to expose and dismantle oppressive gender constructions in visual imagery and discourse.

A somewhat younger generation of women architects and theorists, who had missed the heady years of bra burnings and communes, was deeply influenced by French feminist thinkers, most notably Hélène Cixous, Luce Irigaray, and Julia Kristeva. This group—including Jennifer Bloomer, Beatriz Colomina, and Catherine Ingraham—began to examine subjects closely tied to psychoanalytic and linguistic investigations, such as the construction of self, the gaze, the inscription of binary oppositions and hierarchies within architectural rhetoric.[2] This direction was reinforced by a general interest in French poststructuralist theory among neo-avant-garde architects (notably Peter Eisenman and Bernard Tschumi), although few women (other than Ingraham) explicitly associated themselves with either Derridean philosophy or architectural 'De-constructivism.' At this point, feminism had become fully entrenched in the academy, gaining a certain fashionability and currency—ironically, at a time when feminist writing had become most removed from practice and from politics at large. The writing was often difficult and arcane, and rarely read by professional architects.

Undoubtedly, the seminal event of this second feminist phase was the conference held at Princeton University in 1990, "Sexuality and Space," organized by Beatriz Colomina. With only a third of the speakers trained as architects, the conference introduced to architecture criticism a wide range of perspectives about the construction of sexuality and gender from other fields—art history, anthropology, film, philosophy, psychoanalysis, and sociology. Only one of the participants, Jennifer Bloomer, showed her own designs. Tactile, messy, and constructed of debris, these idiosyncratic assemblages, like Bloomer's rhetorical style, were inspired by the *écriture féminine* of Cixous and Catherine Clément. They could not have been more different from the earnest, socially inspired projects in the *Heresies* issue. Subsequent conferences and publications, such as *Architecture: In Fashion* (1994) and *White Walls, Designer Dresses* (1995), offered detailed analyses of gender constructions in architectural rhetoric, showing how such notions as ornament and structure were closely intertwined with gender hierarchies. And it was this moment that gay and lesbian theoretical writings, notably Henry Urbach's "Closets, Clothes, disClosure" (1996) first appeared on the scene.[3] In contrast to the historical studies of the first feminist phase, which tended to be materialist and social in orientation, and introduced unknown archival material, this second phase focused on rhetoric, often scrutinizing the writings of canonical architects, such as Adolf Loos and Le Corbusier, to gain new perspectives on how gender was inscribed and encoded in their thought. Le Corbusier, whose urban theories had been the focus of Jane Jacobs's devastating critique in the early 1960s, was once again the prime target of attack. Probably no article was published and translated as many times as Colomina's "Battle Lines: E. 1027," which cast Eileen Gray as a victim of Le Corbusier's hubris, jealousy, and spectral and literal defacement.[4]

Partly in reaction to the increasingly rarefied tone and hermetic focus of this phase of critical writing, and partly due to its repetitive and strident message (accusations of sexism and of denigrating the feminine), another approach began to gain prominence in feminist work in the early 1990s. This phase, building on the work on Henri Lefebvre and Michel de Certeau, and revisiting the architecture of the 1950s and 1960s (the Smithsons, Jane Jacobs, Scott Brown and Venturi), examined the everyday experience of women and other marginal groups in terms of both oppression and possibility. Feminism was now seen as part of a broader phenomenon of identity politics, and frequently feminist historical work, such as that of Margaret Crawford, Zeynep Çelik, and Mabel Wilson overlapped with other investigations of identity, whether ethnic, postcolonial, or racial. Indeed, the range and variety of this work, encompassing such topics as women's patronage (Alice Friedman), postwar technology and consumption (Joan Ockman), bodily experience (Deborah Fausch), domesticity and artworks (Sharon Hare), and women architectural critics (Diane Favro, Suzanne Stephens) makes any single characterization nearly impossible. The juncture of these diverse approaches with the social activism of the first phase and the poststructualist, psychoanalytic orientation of the second phase can be seen in the eclectic but stimulating collection, *The Sex of Architecture,* edited by Diana Agrest, Patricia Conway, and Leslie Weisman in 1996.[5] The book of twenty-four essays can be read as a virtual group portrait of American feminist thinking in the mid-1990s—one that crossed generational lines. Shortly thereafter, a flurry of American and British feminist anthologies was published: *Architecture and Feminism* (1996), *The Architect: Reconstructing Her Practice* (1996), *Desiring Practices: Architecture, Gender and the Interdisciplinary* (1996), *Design and Feminism: Revisioning Spaces, Places, and Everyday Things* (1999), and most recently, *Gender Space Architecture* (2000).

If these works signaled a widespread acceptance of feminist concerns, they also, more disturbingly, marked an end point—or so it seemed for nearly fifteen years—of feminism's visibility in American architecture.[6] The flood of publications nearly ground to a halt; few schools continued to offer classes on 'gender and architecture'; and scholars in their twenties or thirties tended to find other subjects— sustainability, digitalization, and globalization— more compelling.

In addition to the larger social and political forces that seem to militate against feminist scholarship, it's very success over three decades may have contributed to its decline.

Names of once forgotten women had been resurrected, the reputations of architecture's male heroes had been taken down a notch or two, and blatant examples of sexual inequity and discrimination in the profession had been exposed, though hardly resolved. Much feminist scholarship and theory had become integrated into other, now mainstream, pursuits.

However, as a new generation of women architects has discovered, many problems remain affecting office practice and the nature of the profession. Likewise, most feminist architecture historians and critics do not view their project as complete, or its viability as dependent upon academic fashion. Survey books and courses continue to make only marginal reference to women practitioners, and few global histories have integrated feminist concerns. There is still much work to be done, and I look forward to new, diverse, and innovative forms of feminist architecture history.

In conclusion, I would like to reflect briefly on early feminist historical writing and to re-examine some

of its methods and premises. These thoughts were sparked by a book I edited on the French designer Charlotte Perriand over fifteen years ago—in fact, just as second-wave feminism seemed to be losing its impetus.[7]

The French designer Charlotte Perriand (1903–99) has often been grouped together with Eileen Gray and Lilly Reich as one of the unsung 'heroes' of the European modern movement, whose design accomplishments have been eclipsed by those of the acknowledged giants: Le Corbusier and Mies van der Rohe. Aside from the three tubular-steel chairs that she designed with Le Corbusier and Pierre Jeanneret as a member of their firm, her work was little known, even though her career spanned three-quarters of a century and extended to locales as diverse as Brazil, Congo, England, France, Japan, French New Guinea, Switzerland, and Vietnam. My initial interest in undertaking this book stemmed from a desire to redress this 'wrong' and to make certain that Perriand's innovative designs would be removed from the shadow of Le Corbusier's towering presence. However, the frequently collaborative nature of her work—like that of Reich, Ray Eames, or Alison Smithson—has made it more difficult to assess her contributions. In addition, like many successful women architects of her generation, Perriand did not wish to perceive herself first and foremost as a woman designer; nor did she particularly identify with the feminist movement in France, complicating efforts to cast her as a 'role model' for contemporary women practitioners. Her career necessitated a more complex reading of the ways that gender intersected with modern architecture than I had originally envisioned, and raised several issues about the assumptions underlying many feminist readings of modern architecture.

The first of these is the tendency to see women architects as victims, whose talent and vital contributions have been suppressed by their male collaborators or associates. This interpretation had a certain strategic value in the 1970s and 1980s, alerting architects to the shortcomings of the 'modern masters' and bringing the issue of gender discrimination to the fore. No doubt there were disturbing inequities in the profession, as is clearly evident in Le Corbusier's oft-quoted, dismissive response to Perriand, "We don't embroider cushions in my atelier," when she first asked him for a job there. However, Perriand's deep admiration of Le Corbusier, her insistence that being a woman did not interfere with her career, and her pleasure in seeing her work as part of a collaborative process all suggest that this characterization of women designers as victims, at least in Perriand's case, has been overstated.

Here, a personal anecdote might be relevant. When I interviewed Perriand in 1997 and mentioned the photograph of her reclining on the chaise longue with her head turned away from the camera, she responded angrily to a question about Beatriz Colomina's reading of the image as representing Le Corbusier's denial of her authorship and creative vision.[8] Perriand told me that she herself had set up the shot, that Pierre Jeanneret took the photo, and that Le Corbusier played no role in its conception, and in fact was in South America at the time. She insisted that it was her choice to turn her head in order to emphasize the chaise rather than its occupant; and that it was also her choice to use that image in her photomontage of the model apartment that she designed with Le Corbusier and Jeanneret for the 1929 Salon d'Automne apartment. Nor was she troubled by the fact that the pivoting chair she designed and displayed on her own was attributed jointly to Le Corbusier-Jeanneret-Perriand, when Thonet began producing the partnership's furniture in 1930. Perriand saw it as an opportunity to have the chair manufactured, and concluded that it would have more impact as part of the atelier's line of tubular-steel furniture: attaining individual recognition as a designer was less important than having the chair regarded as part of a collective vision of modern living. She saw herself as an equal participant with considerable choice and control in her collaboration with Le Corbusier and Jeanneret.

A second issue to consider is the relationship between modern architecture and the entry of women into the profession. Although Le Corbusier was no feminist hero, his atelier seems to have been a place where several women designers chose to work, including Perriand and Stanislavia Nowicki before World War II, and Edith Schreiber, Blanche Limco, and Maria Fenyo immediately afterward. To what extent did the culture of the Modern Movement, and in particular Le Corbusier's commitment to new attitudes and social mores, help foster women's participation in the profession? Did the adventure of creating something new, the Modern Movement's commitment to collective values, and its emphasis on collaboration (however paradoxical, given Le Corbusier's self-proclaimed role as artist-genius) prove especially conducive to strong, independent women? Judging from Perriand's descriptions, not only did she consider herself the equal of the male employees, but she also enjoyed their warmth, camaraderie, and respect. The atelier provided an environment in which she and her colleagues, male and female, could grow and develop professionally.

Third, her salon exhibitions of the late 1920s call into question the stereotypical characterization of modernism as instrumental rationalism, and therefore male. What is evident in her 1928 dining room and the 1929 model apartment, as well as in the broader movement for domestic reform during that decade, was that scientific planning and functionalism were not simply male concerns but were also significant components of women's vision of domestic liberation. Much feminist scholarship has been devoted to the demystification of hierarchical distinctions between attributes such as rationality, functionalism, and structure (traditionally associated with male truth) and characteristics such as decoration, superfluity, and fantasy (associated with a more feminine subjective sensibility), and to disputing the subordination of the latter. But what becomes clear when one examines the interwar discussions about 'scientific' household management is that such a dichotomy is much too simplistic. The domestic-reform movement contributed to the feminization of rationality, just as women (and society at large) increasingly perceived rationality as fundamental to their own identity. The idea that housework could be rationalized and made scientific meant that all women—even homemakers—could see themselves, and be seen, as rational and scientific. Though rarely acknowledged in such terms, the functionalism and rational planning of modern domestic architecture were similarly connected to women's identity. Perriand's salon exhibits in 1928 and 1929 challenge characterizations of both modernism and rationality as exclusively male.

In addition, these projects raise questions about how we characterize feminism or feminist thought. All too often, those of us who are feminist critics and historians evaluate women's historical position by today's standards (whether in terms of individual economic and political rights or from a poststructuralist perspective emphasizing the fluidity of gender and identity). However, if women's struggle for emancipation is to be seen as an evolving, historical phenomenon, it is important to examine earlier, more 'compromised' efforts and to assess them in terms of their own social and political context.

Historian Karen Offen has proposed the term 'relational feminism' to describe the pioneering efforts of many earlier twentieth-century European reformers who attempted to improve women's situation as women, emphasizing their distinctive contributions to society rather than insisting on individual rights, irrespective of sex. These family-oriented feminists rejected the nineteenth-century image of the self-sacrificing *femme au foyer* but, because they believed that there were biological and cultural differences between women and men, still saw women as having primary responsibility for the home and children.[9] In France, prior to the publication of Simone de Beauvoir's *The Second Sex* in 1949, the sexual division of labor was rarely seen as oppressive but rather as part of a necessary complementarity of the sexes. In the view of women domestic reformers such as Paulette Bernège and Henriette Cavaignac, and designers such as Perriand and Le Corbusier, modern technology and scientific planning could liberate women from domestic drudgery, enabling them to use their time in more fulfilling ways, whether in their role as mothers and wives, or pursuing a career, or enjoying leisure activities. Certainly, most visitors to the 1929 *Salon d'Automne* who saw Perriand's kitchen assumed that a woman would be working in it, but the remarks of contemporary critics make clear that many would have also assumed that this woman was a *femme moderne*, forging a new identity both for herself and society.

I would like to see histories of modern architecture explore this apparent paradox, allowing us to include efforts different from our own as part of the rich and diverse history of improving women's condition.

I believe that a deeper knowledge of how gender was constructed, maintained, and challenged would help us address present-day inequities in the profession.

This means going beyond reductive charges of sexism and victimization and simplistic value judgments of good and bad in order to arrive at a fuller, more complex vision of modernism—one that encompasses both its regressive and progressive dimensions.

The last section of this essay was first published as "Perriand: Reflections on Feminism and Modern Architecture," *Harvard Design Magazine*, Stocktaking, no. 20 (2004). Earlier versions of the essay also appeared as "Un sogno rinviato: la storia femminista dell'architettura," *Casabella*, no. 732 (April 4, 2005) and "Um Sonho Adiado: história femista da arquitectura," *Jornal Arquitectos [JA]*, Ser Mulher, no. 242 (July/Aug./Sept. 2011).

Endnotes

1. When I began graduate architecture school in 1972, I was the only woman in my class at Princeton University. By the time, I graduated in 1975, the incoming class was approximately half women. While this was true of many graduate programs on both coasts, there were many schools, especially undergraduate B.Arch. programs, where the percentage of woman students was much smaller. Inequities in other dimensions of the profession, however, have persisted. According to statistics published in *Progressive Architecture* in November 1995, one third of undergraduate and graduate students, 9.1% of regular AIA members, and 8.7% of tenured faculty were women.

2. One should also note in this context the contribution of Diana Agrest, who as a teacher had long discussed psychoanalytic themes and had, from the early 1970s on, exposed students to the writings of French feminists. In addition, one might include in this group two scholars outside of architecture, philosopher Elizabeth Grosz and classicist Ann Bergren, who often participated in architecture conferences in the early 1990s and whose writings were highly influential. Agrest, Grosz, and Bergren are closer in age to the first-phase feminists, but more theoretical in orientation.

3. Henry Urbach, "Closets, Clothes, disClosure," *Assemblage*, no. 30 (August 1996): 62-73. Urbach recalls giving the first version of this paper in 1992 at the sixth Lesbian and Gay Studies Conference, held at Rutgers University in New Brunswick, New Jersey. Urbach, e-mail to the author, March 19, 2019.

4. The first version of Colomina's essay, "War on Architecture: E 1027," is published in a special issue of *Assemblage*, titled *Violence Space*, no. 20 (April 1993), 28-29.

5. Diana Agrest, Patrica Conway, and Leslie Kanes Weisman, eds., *The Sex of Architecture* (New York: Harry N. Abrams, 1996). Two essays in the collection combine materialist and psychoanalytic methodologies, Esther da Costa Meyer's insightful work on agoraphobia and urban space and Diana Agrest's provocative comments on the city and nature.

6. Fortunately, just as the visibility of American feminism seemed to have diminished, feminist historical and theoretical work in Britain gained a new vitality, as evident in such recent events as the conference organized by Vittoria di Palma, Marina Lathouri, and Diana Periton, *The Intimate Metropolis: Domesticating the City, Infiltrating the Room* held at the Architectural Association in London, October 30–November 1, 2003 (a version of which was published in 2009); the numerous publications of the faculty of the Bartlett School at University of London; and books by British architectural historians Elizabeth Darling, Tag Gronberg, Flora Samuel, and Lynne Walker. Conferences in France, Belgium, and the Netherlands suggest this was true in Western Europe as well.

7. Mary McLeod, ed., *Charlotte Perriand: An Art of Living* (New York: Harry N. Abrams, in association with The Architectural League of New York, 2003).

8. Charlotte Perriand, interview with Mary McLeod, June 30, 1997. For Beatriz Colomina's analysis, see "The Split Wall: Domestic Voyeurism," in Colomina, ed., *Sexuality and Space* (New York: Princeton Architectural Press, 1992), 106-7.

9. Karen Offen, "Defining Feminism: A Comparative Historical Approach," *Signs* 14, no. 1 (Autumn 1988): 119-57.

UNFORGETTING WOMEN ARCHITECTS:

A CONFRONTATION WITH HISTORY AND WIKIPEDIA

Despina Stratigakos

History is not a simple meritocracy: it is a narrative of the past written and revised—or not written at all—by people with agendas. This is nothing new; about 3,500 years ago, Thutmose III tried to erase the memory of his dead co-regent, Hatshepsut, one of Egypt's most successful pharaohs and prolific builders, in the most literal of ways: by hacking and scratching her name and image off of her monuments. His motives appear less passionate than political; he may have acted to protect his son, the future Amenhotep II, from rivals to the throne. Amenhotep II, in turn, seized the opportunity during his own reign to expand his legacy by claiming to be the creator of Hatshepsut's defaced works.[1] Many centuries later, such acts of erasure would become known as *damnatio memoriae* after the ancient Roman judgment passed on a person who was condemned not to be remembered. It was a dishonorable fate that the Roman Senate reserved for traitors and tyrants. Today, in modern architectural history, it is simply what we do to women architects.

The reasons we forget women architects are varied and complex. Until recently, historians assumed that there were no female practitioners before the mid-twentieth century, so they did not bother to look for them. Nor was it likely that they would stumble upon these designers by chance, given that traditional research methods focus on archives and libraries, institutions that have been slow to collect women's work.

The International Archive of Women in Architecture, housed at Virginia Tech University in Blacksburg, Virginia, was created in 1985 by Bulgarian architect Milka Bliznakov out of frustration at the enormous loss of material from the first generations of women architects.[2] Few archives wanted their papers, and as these women passed away, decades of drawings, plans, and records ended up in the trash. As a result, anyone seeking to learn about their lives and careers has had to be inventive and eclectic in the use of sources in order to supplement the archival documentation conventionally understood as the historian's primary materials.

Forgetting women architects has also been imbedded in the very models we use for writing architectural history. The monograph format, which has long dominated the field, lends itself to the celebration of the heroic 'genius,' typically a male figure defined by qualities such as boldness, independence, toughness, and vigor—all of which have been coded in Western culture as masculine traits.[3] Moreover, the monograph is usually conceived as a sort of genealogy, which places the architect in a lineage of 'great men,' laying out both the 'masters' from whom he has descended and the impressive followers in his wake. For those seeking to write other kinds of narratives, the monograph has felt like an intellectual straitjacket, especially in contemplating the lives and careers of women that do not fit the prescribed contours.[4] Some of the early histories of women architects used the monographic model to produce a thin substratum of female 'greats,' but they did not thereby challenge the idea that the best architecture is created by mavericks. To be sure, in the past two decades, historians interested in broader, socially based histories have moved away from the monograph's confining format. But it remains powerful and continues to be the bible of the star system. Prominent architects seeking to consolidate their positions in history's pantheon often write or commission their own monographs, projects that are rarely self-critical.[5]

The monograph's insistence on heroic individualism has also discouraged histories about collaborations, as if acknowledging the work of a team would diminish the pot of glory. This has contributed significantly to the forgetting of women architects because it is common for them to work in partnership (for professional and personal reasons), usually with a male who is often also a spouse. Even when a woman has been a full and equal partner, her contribution is rarely recognized as such.[6] The painful negation of Denise Scott Brown in the 1991 awarding of the Pritzker Prize solely to her husband and collaborator, Robert Venturi— which prompted a global petition on Change.org demanding that the Hyatt Foundation, twenty-two years later, set the record straight—is an important, but by no means exceptional, example of how female partners are written out of history by a profession suffering from star architect disorder (a.k.a. SAD).

Scott Brown's case is notable, however, not only because of the controversy it has generated but also because she has been an outspoken critic of her own erasure, bringing attention to the sexism of architecture's star system since long before the Pritzker Prize jury all but sealed her argument with their verdict.[7] But even when women architects have stood up for their own contributions, most historians and prize juries—following the cultural practice of glorifying individual heroes—have usually ignored them, no matter how compelling the evidence of their roles. Using pens rather than chisels, such historians and juries have channeled Thutmose III, removing the names of women architects from their own monuments.

Admittedly, women have sometimes enabled their own disappearance. Male architects do not hesitate to take an active role in preserving their legacies by writing memoirs and ensuring the safe-keeping of their models, drawings, and correspondence. Women—taught that self-promotion is an unattractive female trait—have made less effort to tell their stories. Among older generations, some women in partnerships have chosen to stand in the shadows in order to shine the spotlight on their husbands. Twenty years ago, I spent a day trying to interview a woman architect about her career, which had spanned thirty years, from 1948 to 1978. For the first six years, as a young graduate, she had worked together with her much older husband; after he died, in 1954, she had built a solo career. But every time I asked about *her* projects, she would change the subject to her husband's achievements. After listening politely all morning, I finally told her that I wanted to hear about her contributions as well; she responded that I could only understand her through him (he had been her teacher before becoming her husband), and spent the afternoon telling me even more about her husband and her plans to write a book about him. We never did get around to talking about her work. It was an early lesson in frustration to a graduate student naively determined to rescue women architects from obscurity.

And yet, despite such hurdles, the past few decades have seen a remarkable florescence of books and articles on women architects. These writings have both contributed to and profited from the shift away from the monographic model as well as from increasing dialogue with other disciplines, such as anthropology and philosophy, which have introduced new narrative methods and sources. But although histories of women are now increasingly available, they have yet to become readily *visible*. They rarely appear in course syllabi. Indeed, it is still common in architecture schools for students to complete an entire degree without ever having heard the names of women who practiced before 1970. You cannot walk into a large commercial bookstore, where the design shelves are filled with glossy monographs on international stars, and expect to walk out with a book on a woman architect. Their work is rarely exhibited in major museums, which have shown little interest in their careers or design legacies. In other words, there is a disconnect between the production of histories and their broader dissemination. The books and articles alone have not been enough to build a collective memory that recognizes women architects.

But there is something that we can all do to turn written words into public awareness. Namely, we can intervene to ensure the presence of women architects in online histories, which is increasingly important to do as the web becomes a primary site for making and preserving the cultural record.

Moreover, their current scarcity in the virtual sphere threatens to reinforce the assumption among younger generations that women have not contributed significantly to the profession until very recently. The dearth of entries in the collectively produced free online encyclopedia Wikipedia, one of the most visited websites in the world, is particularly worrisome. But it is not just women architects who are missing. Although women comprise half of Wikipedia's readers, they are dramatically underrepresented among the ranks of the site's editors: only nine percent of the site's editors were women in 2012, down from thirteen percent in 2010. Not surprisingly, the gender gap among editors is reflected in a gender gap in content; male editors write about subjects with which they are familiar and that interest them.[8] Sue Gardner, then executive director of the Wikimedia Foundation, pledged to raise the number of women editors, while admitting that the website's culture resists female participation.[9] Women editors who submit new entries on women's history routinely find that male editors question their sources and the significance of their topics and are quick to nominate such entries for deletion. In a March 2012 edit-a-thon, "She Blinded Me with Science," held at the Smithsonian to add notable female scientists, entries were nominated for deletion almost as soon as they were posted.[10]

In 2013, I witnessed this kind of editorial hassling in action when someone tried to post about the architect Thekla Schild on the German Wikipedia site.[11] I had discovered Schild in the course of my dissertation research and had written about her efforts, in the years before the First World War, to integrate the architecture program of the Karlsruhe Institute of Technology. Schild's story is noteworthy not just because of her success in opening up the program to women (she was only the second woman in Germany to earn an architecture degree) but also because she wrote a memoir of the experience. Such firsthand accounts of academic integration are unusual in any field; in architecture, they are extremely rare. Schild's manuscript, which was never published, provides insights into what architectural education was like a century ago and how society viewed the status of architects.[12]

Given my prior interest, I noticed when, early in the morning of March 30, 2013, an editor with the user name CMdibev posted a brief entry on Schild. This editor, new to Wikipedia, had earlier in the same month posted numerous times on historical female figures, including on other women architects. Yet just thirteen minutes after the initial post on Schild appeared, a male editor, Der Krommodore, who has been posting on the site since 2008, had marked the article for immediate deletion (without the seven-day grace period for discussion usually afforded new entries). Admittedly, the entry on Schild seemed hastily written and was incomplete, and some of the criticisms were valid. But two things caught my eye (and raised my blood pressure): first, Der Krommodore asserted that Schild was not sufficiently accomplished to be listed on Wikipedia; and second, he expressed doubt that Schild *had ever existed*. During nearly twenty years of writing about women architects, I have certainly encountered dismissive attitudes toward the topic, but no one had ever denied the actual existence of my subjects. Der Krommodore, who identified himself as a Bavarian interested in linguistics as well as a monarchist and cigar-smoking, cognac-swilling insomniac, had Googled Schild and, finding nothing, assumed she was fictional. Eventually another editor told Der Krommodore to back off and give CMdibev time to complete the entry, but the latter seemed to give up. Over the next few weeks, however, other editors, in the kind of collaborative work that Wikipedia encourages, completed a detailed entry, thus saving Schild and baptizing her into the virtual world. Still, the ease with which Der Krommodore could dismiss Schild was stunning—and this is exactly why ensuring the virtual presence of past women architects matters so much. As Mia Ridge, a young scholar and proponent of digital histories, argues, search engines are now shaping our conception of the world.

A historian might spend decades undertaking research in archives and writing up discoveries in scholarly journals, but if the work does not have a presence online—and, specifically, a presence that is not behind a paywall—it is all but invisible outside academia.

Ridge puts the dilemma plainly: "If it's not Googleable, it doesn't exist."[13] And because Wikipedia articles usually show up first in Google search rankings, intervening on the site is especially important in establishing online visibility.

Just how much information and history are missing from Wikipedia becomes clear in comparison to the free, user-generated digital archive of American female architects created by the Beverly Willis Architecture Foundation (BWAF). The Dynamic National Archive, or DNA, includes over 1,100 practitioners from all fifty states, and it is still growing.[14] Wikipedia's "List of Female Architects," by comparison, includes in its United States category 114 female architects from some twenty-five states, but even these numbers are misleading because, of those 114 entries, thirty-six, or a third, have no content at all (one links to the entry of a man with a similar name).[15] The DNA, too, has many entries that still need to be completed. Like Wikipedia, the BWAF relies on the public to build the database but it also reaches out to experts to edit or to add entries. The BWAF is currently working on a National Endowment for the Arts–sponsored initiative, "Women of 20th-Century American Architecture," involving fifty scholars (I am one of them) who are researching and posting entries on fifty women chosen by a jury; this work will become part of its online collection. Although the BWAF archive does not rank as highly in Google searches as Wikipedia, some of the Wikipedia entries on American women architects cite it in their sources; adding more such links would increase the traffic between the sites.

The existence of female lists on Wikipedia arguably undermines the goal of integrating knowledge about women on the website. In April 2013, American novelist Amanda Filipacchi set off a fierce debate with her *New York Times* opinion piece about how Wikipedia's editors were quietly restructuring its categories to exclude women. "I just noticed something strange on Wikipedia," she wrote. "It appears that gradually, over time, editors have begun the process of moving women, one by one, alphabetically, from the 'American Novelists' category to the 'American Women Novelists' subcategory." The intention, she surmised, was to create an all-male "American Novelists" category.[16] As Joyce Carol Oates tweeted in response, "All (male) writers are writers; a (woman) writer is a woman writer."[17] A few days later, technology author James Gleick, reporting on the growing controversy for the *New York Times Book Review* blog, noted that it was becoming apparent that the problem was broader and more pervasive than had first appeared. "Throughout Wikipedia, in all kinds of categories, women and people of nonwhite ethnicities are assigned only to their subcategories," he wrote. "Maya Angelou is in African-American writers, African-American women poets, and American women poets, but not American poets or American writers."[18]

Wikipedia's main "List of Architects," which spans the period from antiquity to the present, includes 755 architects. Of these, 726 are men and only twenty-nine are women. Although male architects admittedly have had a larger presence in the field than women, the imbalance here is also the result of who participates in Wikipedia. Obscure male architects with few accomplishments are included, whereas one looks in vain for the names of more distinguished and influential female practitioners, such as Marion Mahony Griffin, Charlotte Perriand, Eileen Gray, Jeanne Gang, and others. Moreover, architectural practice is traditionally defined with a focus on the individual creator. This is why we find Robert Venturi listed under twentieth-century architects, but not Denise Scott Brown.[19]

I am not certain that the solution to the absence of women from the general "List of Architects" would be to simply merge that category with the "List of Female Architects," as was urged by many Wikipedians for "American Novelists" and the newly created subcategory "American Women Novelists" shortly after Filipacchi's piece appeared.[20] Wikipedia has many such lists concerning women, ranging from politicians in the United States Congress and CEOs of Fortune 500 companies to models on the *Price Is Right* television show. Not all of them are empowering, or meant to be. But there is something to be said for those cases, as with architecture, where women's contributions are so little known that a collection makes a point in and of itself—it visualizes a presence and a legacy, however hastily sketched out. At the same time, as Filipacchi points out, people "go to Wikipedia to get ideas for whom to hire, or honor, or read," and if they stumble first on the general page, as is most likely to happen, they may never realize that the women are missing.[21] For this reason, women will remain half-hidden if they appear solely on the "List of Female Architects."

The phenomenal attention garnered by the Scott Brown petition testifies not only to the power of the Internet and the support for her cause but also to a widespread dissatisfaction with the ongoing invisibility of women's accomplishments. In June 2013, when I first published an article in *Places Journal* on the threat of women architects' being yet again written out of history, now digitally, my call to action tapped into that discontent.[22] Later that year, *East of Borneo*, an online art magazine based in Los Angeles, hosted the first edit-a-thon to write women architects into Wikipedia, citing my article and the Denise Scott Brown petition controversy as their sources of inspiration.[23] In mid-May 2014, Arielle Assouline-Lichten, who, along with Caroline James, had instigated the petition, organized her own Wikipedia edit-a-thon at Storefront for Art and Architecture in New York City as part of a larger "Digital Invisibles" event devoted to increasing the online presence of marginalized histories in architecture.[24] Despite the pleasant weather and the lure of Central Park and other attractions that warm Saturday afternoon, eager would-be Wikipedians crowded the room.

Upholding the Internet's democratic potential, each of us can be a part of the effort to unforget a woman architect. Consider reading a book or an article on a woman architect and contributing what you have learned to the DNA (it is user-friendly, and there are no censorious Krommodores patrolling the premises) or to Wikipedia (numerous websites give tips on how to edit). Reach out to friends and colleagues with laptops and organize an edit-a-thon. And, if you are an educator, make Wikipedia-editing a class assignment.

Contributing to Wikipedia and other online databases represents a real opportunity to provide students and younger readers as well as the larger public with a more accurate perception of women's participation in architecture.

There is also something very satisfying about writing a forgotten figure—a professional ancestor, maybe even a pioneer—into history. And with each entry, the long and rich legacy of women in architecture grows brighter, making it that much harder to ignore women in architecture, whether in the classroom, in the museum, or on prize juries.

As Sue Gardner of Wikimedia put it, "Wikipedia will only contain 'the sum of all human knowledge' if its editors are as diverse as the population itself: you can help make that happen. And I can't think of anything more important to do, than that."[25]

Republished with permission of Princeton University Press, from [*Where are the Women Architects?*, Despina Stratigakos, 2016]; permission conveyed through Copyright Clearance Center, Inc.

This chapter draws on and expands an earlier article: Despina Stratigakos, "Unforgetting Women Architects: From Pritzker to Wikipedia," *Places Journal*, June 2013, http://places.designobserver.com/feature/unforgetting-women-architects-from-pritzker-to-wikipedia/37912.

Endnotes

1 On Hatshepsut, see Kara Cooney, *The Woman Who Would Be King: Hatshepsut's Rise to Power in Ancient Egypt* (New York: Crown, 2014), and Catharine H. Roehrig, Renée Dreyfus and Cathleen A. Keller, eds., *Hatshepsut, From Queen to Pharaoh* (New York: Metropolitan Museum of Art, and New Haven, CT: Yale University Press, 2005).

2 International Archive of Women in Architecture, http://spec.lib.vt.edu/IAWA, accessed May 25, 2015.

3 Christine Battersby, *Gender and Genius: Toward a Feminist Aesthetics* (London: Women's Press, 1989).

4 Natalie Kampen and Elizabeth G. Grossman, "Feminism and Methodology: Dynamics of Change in the History of Art and Architecture" (Working Paper no. 1212, Center for Research on Women, Wellesley College, Wellesley, MA, 1983), 9 ff; Cheryl Buckley, "Made in Patriarchy: Towards a Feminist Analysis of Women and Design," *Design Issues* 3 (Autumn 1986): 10–12; Abigail A. Van Slyck, "Women in Architecture and the Problems of Biography," *Gender and Design*, special issue, *Design Book Review* 25 (Summer 1992): 19–22.

5 Amanda Baillieu, "Architecture Is the Loser if We Censor History: Monographs Contribute to the Marginalisation of the Profession," *BDonline*, January 30, 2015, accessed March 22, 2019, http://www.bdonline.co.uk/comment/architecture-is-the-loser-if-we-censor-history/5073506.article.

6 Helen Searing et al., "Equal and Unequal Partners, 1881–1970," in *Equal Partners: Men and Women Principals in Contemporary Architectural Practice* (Northampton, MA: Smith College Museum of Art, 1998), 22–39.

7 Denise Scott Brown, "Room at the Top: Sexism and the Star System in Architecture," in *Architecture: A Place for Women*, ed. Ellen Perry Berkeley and Matilda McQuaid (Washington, DC: Smithsonian Institution Press, 1989), 237–46.

8 Claire Potter, "Prikipedia? Or, Looking for the Women on Wikipedia," *Chronicle of Higher Education*, (March 10, 2013), http://chronicle.com/blognetwork/tenuredradical, retrieved January 20, 2015.

9 Noam Cohen, "Define Gender Gap? Look Up Wikipedia's Contributor List," *New York Times*, January 30, 2011; Sue Gardner, "Nine Reasons Women Don't Edit Wikipedia (in Their Own Words)," *Sue Gardner's Blog*, February 19, 2011, http://suegardner.org /2011/02/19/nine-reasons-why-women-dont-edit-wikipedia-in-their-own-words, accessed January 20, 2015.

10 Potter, "Prikipedia?"; Aviva Shen, "How Many Women Does It Take to Change Wikipedia?" *Smithsonian*, April 4, 2012, http://www.smithsonianmag.com/smithsonian -institution/how-many-women-does-it-take-to-change-wikipedia-171400755 /?no-ist=.

11 "Thekla Schild," *Wikipedia*, accessed January 20, 2015, https://de.wikipedia.org/wiki/Thekla_Schild.

12 Despina Stratigakos, "'I Myself Want to Build:' Women, Architectural Education and the Integration of Germany's Technical Colleges," *Paedagogica Historica* 43, no. 6 (2007): 727–56.

13 Mia Ridge, "New Challenges in Digital History: Sharing Women's History on Wikipedia," paper delivered at the Women's History in the Digital World Conference, Bryn Mawr College, Bryn Mawr, PA, March 23, 2013, http://repository.brynmawr.edu /greenfield_conference/papers/saturday/37.

14 Dynamic National Archive Collection, Beverly Willis Architecture Foundation, accessed May 25, 2015, http://www.bwaf.org/dna.

15 "List of Female Architects," *Wikipedia*, accessed January 21, 2015, https://en.wikipedia.org/wiki/List_of_female_architects.

16 Amanda Filipacchi, "Wikipedia's Sexism Toward Female Novelists," *New York Times*, April 24, 2013.

17 Joyce Carol Oates (@JoyceCarolOates), "@ecshowalter Wikipedia bias an accurate reflection of universal bias. All (male) writers are writers; a (woman) writer is a woman writer," Twitter, April 25, 2013, 7:27 a.m., https://twitter.com/JoyceCarolOates/status/327428620895272962.

18 Joyce Carol Oates, quoted by James Gleick, "Wikipedia's Women Problem," *New York Review of Books Blog*, April 29, 2013, http://www.nybooks.com/blogs/nyrblog/2013/apr/29/wikipedia-women-problem.

19 "List of Architects," *Wikipedia*, accessed January 21, 2015, https://en.wikipedia.org/wiki/List_of_architects.

20 Gleick, "Wikipedia's Women Problem."

21 Filipacchi, "Wikipedia's Sexism Toward Female Novelists."

22 Despina Stratigakos, "Unforgetting Women Architects: From Pritzker to Wikipedia," *Places Journal*, June 2013, http:// places.designobserver.com/feature/unforgetting-women-architects-from-pritzker-to-wikipedia/37912.

23 *East of Borneo*, "Unforgetting L.A. #2: MAK Center for Art and Architecture," event held December 14, 2013, http://www.eastofborneo.org/unforgetting2, retrieved January 21, 2015.

24 Storefront for Art and Architecture, "Wwwriting Series: Digital Invisibles," May 17, 2014, accessed March 22, 2019, http://www.storefrontnews.org/archive/2010?y=0&m=0&p=0&c=10&e=616,. The edit-a-thon event was also part of a broader exhibition held at the Storefront for Art and Architecture, *Letters to the Mayor*, which asked fifty architects (among them, two men) to write letters expressing concerns about the future of urban landscapes to political leaders worldwide.

25 Sue Gardner, comment made on November 24, 2010, on "Unlocking the Clubhouse: Five Ways to Encourage Women to Edit Wikipedia," *Sue Gardner's Blog*, November 14, 2010, http://suegardner.org/2010/11/14/unlocking-the-clubhouse-five-ways-to-encourage-women-to-edit-wikipedia/#comments.

BEING FIRST

CONVERSATION BETWEEN SADIE MORGAN + SAMANTHA HARDINGHAM

AA XX 100 was a project to celebrate the centenary of women at the Architectural Association (AA) in London, England from 1917-2017. The culmination of this project took place in autumn 2017 with a major exhibition about contributions by AA women to the profession, a collection of historical and critical writings, and an international conference organized by the AA in collaboration with the Paul Mellon Centre at the AA. The following conversation between Samantha Hardingham and Sadie Morgan was the opening keynote of the conference. Titled "Being First," the conversation reflected on the fact that Hardingham and Morgan have been pioneers in their achievements, breaking new ground for women in architecture. While this is exciting and something to be celebrated, it also makes us question why it has taken so long for women to be able to contribute and be recognized in such varied ways within architecture and its related disciplines. (Introduction by Manijeh Verghese)

SH When Sadie and I had the conversation about what we might talk about, it was apparent that one of the things we have in common is that we both grew up in Kent. We are both Good Women of Kent, the Garden of England. So yes, this is a very international school, but we happen to come from a very small part of England, which I thought was quite interesting. And so, I thought, being in the mode of having just finished my book on Cedric Price which was arranged chronologically, I am in a chronological frame of mind. So this is where we will begin, particularly in one of the comments you've made Sadie, about advocating for the importance of design that connects people back to place. And so, I wanted to start by connecting you back to the place where you grew up. How formative was your childhood?

SM I was brought up in a commune in Sevenoaks, of all places. This was sort of an anathema because my communist grandfather picked the most Tory stronghold in the whole of the United Kingdom. I spent a long time thinking it didn't have much to do with the way I formed my career and my thinking, but actually it was totally fundamental. And the interesting thing about being brought up in a place where your parents don't have to be responsible for everything, is that you learn very quickly that you need a group of people around you with different perspectives. If you can learn from those different perspectives, then you come out feeling much better about yourself because you can generally pick the person who's going to teach you the things that you want to learn. You also have a very clear sense of the importance of looking after each other. A sense of responsibility towards others. The commune was set up by three professional families who decided that they would put all their money into one large house and they would all live and eat together. So, the rule was one room per person and my grandfather was a psychiatrist who had a lot of gay and single mothers who he would look after. Throughout his career, we would have his patients come and live within the community and he believed very

strongly that women should be able to go out to work. He had a nursery and I went to that nursery while my mother went out to work. As I grew up, I was surrounded by a nuclear physicist who lived above me and who I would chat with if I had a problem with my homework: if I needed to smoke a cigarette and talk about sex I would go to the barmaid who lived in the flat across the way. I also had a huge sense of responsibility because from the age of five or six, I would come home after school and look after my great grandmother who by the time she died, was 111—the oldest woman in Great Britain and not thanks to my care. You know, I still feed the very elderly lady who lives across the way every Sunday night. My children have grown up understanding this, and I have the most extraordinary independent young women who judge nobody. They are completely capable of having a conversation with an older person or a young person. And it's a very special way of growing up I think.

SH So, you continue to live in that way in the commune with your own family?

SM Yes, I never left. Many people keep pointing to the fact that I never left home. I would say it is a really interesting social model as we

---

FIGURE 1. Samantha Hardingham and Sadie Morgan in conversation at the AA XX 100 keynote. Photography courtesy of the Architectural Association Photo Library.

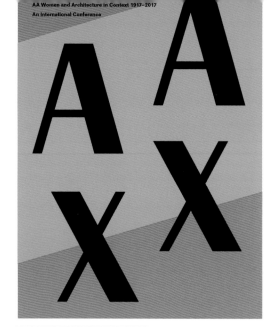

AA Women and Architecture in Context 1917–2017
An International Conference

FIGURE 2. AA XX 100: AA WOMEN AND ARCHITECTURE IN CONTEXT 1917-2017 Conference Programme 2-4 November 2017. Courtesy of the AA Print Studio.

move towards a future where we are going to have a much larger elderly population. We have more diverse sets of communities today. How do we as a society encourage generosity? How do we encourage a sense of community that if we're not careful, we can lose? If you look at what's happening around the world it's quite frightening.

SH That might encourage me to ask about many of the housing projects that you've worked on, but I will hold back for a moment. We will come back to that, because now I am intrigued about how you then went on and studied architecture.

SM I studied interiors at Kingston and then I went to the Royal College of Art and studied interior architecture there.

SH And the decision to do that— was it something you knew you wanted to do, or was it a question of "I can do that?"

SM It's funny because I sort of fell into it. I seem to fall into most things, but that might just be a subconscious view. I studied arts, physics, and biology, and because I hadn't studied chemistry—having gone to a good grammar school—there was

no ambition other than to be a legal secretary, as opposed to a secretary. I actually didn't have the combination of grades to go and become a doctor. So I was a bit stuck. No one really knew what to do with me. Nowadays, I take heart that young women are encouraged to go for professions that were just not considered in the past.

SH Was it a case of finding something that you enjoyed doing or was there somebody that inspired you and made you realize you were interested in design?

SM Well my father was an architect and came to the AA and my mother was a designer. So, I think that I've always been in a family that believed that design mattered. In a sense, there's always been a huge pressure to go towards an academic career. Yet, I never felt any pressure at all about what it was that I would do. I think for young men and women today there is this pressure to absolutely know what you are going to do and how you are going to get there. Yet for me, I had no plan and no way to get there.

SH Talking about plans, you somehow made a plan and set up a practice. How did that happen?

SM The irony is that with my tutor Alex de Rijke, and Philip Marsh with whom I went to college, we were invited to submit some work for the Architecture Foundation's ten new architecture practices. Because we had all slightly collaborated doing different things, we submitted a collection of work, for which we got picked as one of the ten. And on the back of that, there was a competition to design a building for the LDDC (London Docklands Development Corporation) as it was called back then and we won that as well. None of us were qualified, we were just mates who suddenly had to formulate a practice. So, we went home and I said, "Dad can I use your professional indemnity?" which is not

60

a normal request for a daughter. He said yes, but then very tragically that summer when we were designing it, dad died very unexpectedly of a heart attack and we were forced into a very different plan. I think my life's been a little bit like that ever since. We put ourselves together as a practice and basically ran our practice from the room downstairs here at the AA: we would have meetings up in the bar. The AA is absolutely wonderful to enable you to do things like that. In our spare time and evenings, we would come and use the studio space and then when people started to notice, we thought we'd better get legitimate and get our own place. So it was an extraordinary time and one that was just full of exploration and absolutely no money. But that's very freeing. I remember getting our first 1,000 pounds, literally after about nine months of working, and we were like "Ohhhh 300 pounds each!"

SH Your first building was with Roger Zogolovich, which was also an interesting collaboration as Roger was a developer and former president of the AA. Would you call it a collaboration?

SM Yes, very much so. Roger is an incredible patron of young people and actually the most extraordinarily lovely person to work with. We learned a lot from each other. I think for any architect who becomes a developer, it's very difficult to stand back and not get involved. But actually, in this instance, it was good because we had never built in concrete before. To be working with someone who understood architecture was fantastic. I adore Roger.

SH In terms of forming a set of design themes, tropes, or values within the practice, did the projects choose you or did you choose the projects?

SM It was a bit of both. We had a fascination with materials and using off-the-shelf resources carefully and inventively. We tended to be given

very complex problems with very small budgets, which is a wonderful place to start because then all you can do is be inventive and problem solve. Then, after a while, you look at all these people who've got these incredible projects with big budgets and you gaze into the distance and think "Oh, wouldn't that be nice?" But you soon realize that actually what matters to you is delivering projects that you've chosen. We did a lot of social housing and a lot of schools; they don't tend to have big budgets and that's fine. You take your pleasure and your pride from designing great spaces. Better classrooms, a good public realm, community buildings; all the things that actually matter in creating a better society. If you ever have the chance to do something better, or more thoughtfully, or more robustly, then that's the thing. I think as a practice, we naturally fell into that way of working because we all very strongly believe in society.

SH Was it a collective belief, and, do the partners have specialties?

SM When we first started working together, Alex used to say he was the head, I was the heart, and Philip was the hands. At that time, we had different skills and slightly different interests. Alex is absolutely obsessed with materials, wood in particular, while Philip is very clear that his skill

set is planning and putting things together. I tend to draw people and ideas together. I think this naturally becomes the glue that holds these things together. All three of us have huge input on the intellectual capital of what we produce.

SH That very naturally leads you to doing all the other things you do alongside practice. You are currently chair of the independent design panel for High Speed Two (HST), member of the National Infrastructure Commission UK, member of the Thames Estuary 2050 growth commission, Mayor's design advocate for Greater London Authority, and professor at Westminster University. So, to go from the scale of the house to national infrastructure, is it all the same?

SM It's funny. I'll tell you the story about HST because it's quite interesting for today. When I concluded my presidency at the AA, I felt that it would be good to do something similar. I had been involved with putting together the design vision for HST and a friend phoned up and said, "Do you know that they are looking for a chair?" I said, "Oh no I didn't." And so, I phoned up and said, "Could you tell me in which paper I can find the job description?" and they said, "We'll get back to you." Nothing happened for a day or two,

FIGURE 3. Prof. Sadie Morgan, Founding Director of dRMM. © Andy Matthews.

and then I got a call saying, "Yes, we will send you the job description." When I received the job description and looked at it, I felt physically sick. I thought there was no way I would get it because the description said, "You must know this and you must do this, and so forth." And I read it and thought, how embarrassing, "What am I going to say now?" And my absolutely lovely office manager at the time read it and said, "Oh Sadie, you can do that standing on your head!" So, I rewrote my CV accordingly, handed it back in, and then I didn't hear anything. I eventually heard that the main head-hunter wanted to see it. And it was then that this unbelievably awful man phoned me and said, "You do realize what a high-profile job this is? You do realize that you will be expected to talk to politicians at the highest level?" I thought to myself, "Don't you tell me what to do." The rest of the conversation did not go very well until he interviewed me. Then he decided that maybe I could be the deputy. The other two on the shortlist were Sirs, yet I was given an interview and had absolutely nothing to lose. I was asked during the interview, "What do you think of our design vision?" And I answered, "What design vision? Have you looked at how awful the website looks?" By the end of it, they must have thought, "Just shut this woman up and give her the job." But in all seriousness, I think they realized that they needed to be told something different and they needed to be given a different perspective. It

has been the most incredible journey and I absolutely love it. I feel it is very important to do.

SH That idea that there's nothing to lose is fantastic. It's partly determination, but it also speaks to the idea that if you try to put me off, that just makes me want something even more.

SM Once that switch is turned on, you actually truly begin to understand your value. I didn't understand my value until I was invited to sit on the National Infrastructure Commission. I arrived at my first meeting and I had Lord Heseltine sitting next to me and Lord Adonis sitting opposite me. Demissis Abbis, who I believe to be the next Einstein, and Tim Besley, chief economist to the World Bank, were also there. I just sat there thinking I don't feel great about this. And then the Chancellor of the Exchequer walked in and I thought, "I think I'm going to throw up. Get me out of this room." The Chancellor then said, "I'm going to go around the table and I'd like you to tell me what you think of the national infrastructure commission." I had gotten the papers the night before and hadn't really had much of a chance to read them. Anyway, it was absolutely fine. And every time I went to a Commissioner's meeting after that I would think, "What is it that I can offer?" After the second or third meeting I understood what I could offer, which is this: while there's a lot of big strategic thinking

that happens, very few people have the capability of bringing that thinking to a level that touches people and places; who can talk about things in a way that considers what it means to normal people and our environment. These are people who understand that if you're going to invest in something, then you have to think about the wider benefits, and that's not always cash.

SH Given this definition of architecture and the ability to present your ideas, and to know very clearly what your role is and how to articulate it, were you ever tempted to draw it out in order to understand it—to literally make a drawing? Or is it a different design pursuit?

SM No, it's exactly the same design pursuit in that you are solving problems. It's a very three-dimensional activity and I have the capability to do this in my head. It's a skill I've learned over time, because you have to learn to make big strategic, important decisions very quickly. As architects, we are constantly doing this. I was taught a very different way of working in which if you have a problem, you unpick it, work it out, take a look at it, and then come back to it again. I nearly always came back to the same first thing I did, even if you take a long time to think about whether that was the right solution. The irony is that when you're making much bigger complex decisions you tend to have a much shorter time frame to do so. You have all the information condensed in front of you, and you have to take this information and analyze it very quickly to come up with a decision. There's a lot of pressure around this process, but it's also hugely exciting and involves the same type of thinking but in a very different form.

FIGURE 4. AA XX 100 Exhibition opening. Photography courtesy of the Architectural Association Photo Library.

FIGURE 5. AA XX 100 Exhibition at 36 Bedford Square. Photography courtesy of the Architectural Association Photo Library.

SH Making big strategic decisions can be a difficult thing to do—certainly it carries a lot of responsibility. Do you have a reference point or people you admire?

SM I admire a great number of people, yet they tend not to be people I would necessarily suggest to my peers. I have a huge amount of respect for my peers, and those who work in my office. I respect a whole group of people for different things. I was once asked, "Who is your inspiration?" and I said, "Michelle Obama." Anybody who can be such a public profile standing next to the most powerful man in the world is somebody I respect. And that sounded a bit glib because I don't always tend to have an answer to this question, as I tend to take inspiration from those around me. The thing I really think a lot about at the moment is that you have to create something that is stronger than the sum of its parts. And because there are so little resources around, I find that in all the work that I do for the National Infrastructure Commission and the HST, I think: "How do you put together a group of people or create a group of ideas that somehow, because they are combined, are much, much better because of it?"

SH So, I actually do have a hero, so much so in fact I wrote a book about him. In a way you remind me a lot of him—Cedric Price. While you don't look anything like him, you behave quite like him and there are two very interesting parallels.

SM I am totally flattered.

SH Cedric was a great champion of women. In fact, he was the only man who was allowed to go to the National Women's Conference—this was in the early 1980s. They let him in because he was always interested in championing the people around him. He also did a lot of work on the infrastructure for the Channel Tunnel link going from Stratford; the strategic thinking in and around connections and moments of arrival and departure, which of course is invisible work. It is invisible work in a sense, but it also has a twenty-five-year lifespan of just the thinking and planning part, before any physical impact is made. There is a parallel in that scale of working, and then there is the Pier. The prize-winning Pier, which I think Alex, described as a bit of a Cedric project, because there is not much building. So, I wonder how much of that thinking clearly resonates in your practice?

SM Well we don't plan it that way. That's just the way it happens. If you look at Hastings Pier, which I have to say is an extraordinary project because 'less is more' in this instance, the project is about listening to the architect as curator rather than builder. The way in which that project came about was all about collaboration and all about restraint. They wanted an iconic building at the end of the pier, and as an architecture practice, that's what you want to do. But then you realize that it's absolutely the wrong solution. The right solution, as Alex has been quoted as saying, was to do nothing but make a service platform on which anything could happen. It offers a huge opportunity for local residents and the community. I believe very strongly that design isn't just about aesthetics, it's about problem solving. And we have to understand better, as students and architects, what our skill sets are. I think that in five, ten, and fifteen years' time, the way that we will work and operate will be completely different, yet we are very slow in picking this up. We are in a place where algorithms are now designing structure; all motorway signage is put on structures designed not by people, but by algorithms. I'm not suggesting that's necessarily something we can say will happen to our buildings, but we have to be seen as relevant to a conversation that begins much earlier on. I think that as things are changing so quickly, we as a profession have to get wise and get in early. We have to convince politicians and big organizations that architects, designers, and creative thinkers have a place at the table. We have this huge skill, we can look into the future, and we can imagine. In doing so we have an opportunity to actually create our future, which most people aren't capable of doing. So, my big push at the moment is to convince politicians and the national infrastructure—which I think I've done—to say "You need creative people." There's a recommendation in the interim report that we put together a group of designers and thinkers who will help support all national infrastructure and commissions. When 200 billion pounds of money will be spent over the next twenty years, if we're not careful, none of us will be involved in that because it's a different type of built environment being designed.

SH There's a brilliant quote by Winnifred Rial, who was one of the first four women at the AA, who said, "In the near future, the women architect will not only be a vague possibility but an absolute necessity." I would say that you know every team needs a good woman and you're proof of that.

FIGURE 6. AA XX 100 Conference keynote at 36 Bedford Square. Photography courtesy of the Architectural Association Photo Library.

Shaping Polemics investigates narratives of action, empowerment, and contestation. While women make up close to half of enrolled architecture students in many schools of architecture, they continue to account for a far smaller percentage of licensed architects. By all indications women continue to reject the traditional role of practice at a far greater rate than their male colleagues. Why is this the case and what results from this implicit rejection of the traditional definition of the profession? Where do these highly educated architects choose to practice and what alternative careers do they pursue? Each of the three papers included in this section ask how and why women identify alternate venues for their work, enquiry, and creativity. For when they do, their work re-appears in unexpected venues not traditionally associated with the discipline. Brown makes a compelling argument for empowering the spaces of women as a form of political advocacy, Moskovitz contributes a vision of grass-roots advocacy that greatly expands the architect's typical remit, and Pitts offers sobering statistics of gender disparities still present in the profession.

shaping
polemics

STATUS QUO

Lori Brown

When I think about the discipline of architecture, status quo is one of the first descriptors that comes to mind. According to the *Oxford English Dictionary*, status quo is defined as "the existing state of affairs 'that maintains, or is committed to maintaining, the existing state of affairs.'"[1] Architecture has an ongoing slowness, even unwillingness to change. Clearly there are those within architectural education and practice who are invested in maintaining the status quo, keeping things the way they are. If the discipline seriously wanted to change, it would have done so by now. We can look to other male dominated disciplines, for example medicine and law, that have made greater inroads with diversifying their ranks than architecture.[2]

However, there are many of us that are working to create change within the discipline of architecture. This text discusses several aspects of my work that challenge the status quo and seek to change the discipline and its engagement with broader social and political issues. I work to expand the discipline to be more politically engaged and relevant to the broader public and raise awareness about our built environment, and the influences directly shaping it. My work in the academy and out in the world disrupts the status quo and seeks to create a different discipline.

I am a feminist, architect, academic, and activist. I use feminist methods to both disrupt power structures and reveal power inequalities.[3]

I question what is assumed architectural 'universal' knowledge and who produces this knowledge. What may first appear as neutral knowledge, is generally not neutral. Knowledge production is shaped by an individual's own education, cultural influences, and social and political positioning. Feminist methods consider larger forces that influence one's positionality. Feminist methods work to re-contextualize and re-politicize knowledge and knowledge production.[4] Feminist scholarship is interested in issues of subjectivity, identity, and the body, as well as how sexual difference reflects power relations. As feminist geographer Linda McDowell has written, people are "culturally shaped and historically and spatially positioned."[5]

I would like to take a moment and discuss what I mean by feminist because there is often confusion around this word.

Feminist practices are political acts that seek to challenge the status quo and identified relationships of power,[6] as argued by some feminist geographers.

One of the many potentials these geographers see in using a feminist methodology is that of "an open and dynamic knowledge community."[7] One that is more accessible by the broader public. I must dispel the belief that feminism is only about women. Although the feminist movement began with the vested interest in women's rights and equality by middle class white women, this movement has expanded to encompass broader issues of social justice and equality for women in the broadest sense of the term and all under-privileged and under-represented peoples.

0: Intersectional Feminism

Intersectional feminism is a term coined by legal scholar Kimberle Crenshaw, in the late 1980s and early 1990s, which argues that intersectionality:

denote[s] the various ways in which race and gender interact to shape the multiple dimensions of Black [people's lives].[8]

She hopes through this methodology

to disrupt the tendencies to see race and gender as exclusive or separable … [and that] the concept can and should be expanded by factoring in issues such as class, sexual orientation, age, and color. [9]

In an interview with legendary African-American activist Angela Davis for the *Women of the World* series, she discusses what she sees as an intersectional feminism on the rise in 2017, one defined by Black women. She argues that intersectionality is an activist endeavor—one that is yet to be really 'figured out.' This framework does bring together multiple modes of oppression enabling more nuanced understanding of people's lives and the structural inequalities faced by so many.[10] The current feminist movement is deeply indebted to intersectional feminism and the future of progressive change will not move forward without intersectional approaches.

FIGURE 1. Private Choices Public Spaces 2014 poster. Image courtesy of the author.

The Women's March in January 2017 is an important example of how intersectional feminism can harness a heterogeneous approach to the myriad issues confronting us today. Architecture has much to learn from such approaches both within the academy and out in practice.

1: Politics of Space

The first research area I discuss is the politics of space. The impetus of both my research and broader engagement is my frustration with the lack of political participation by the discipline of architecture, at large. I have been, and continue to be, compelled to investigate topics that remain unavoidably political. In this particular case, the primary focus is landscapes of reproductive healthcare access in North America. *Contested Spaces: Abortion Clinics, Women's Shelters and Hospitals* seeks to make explicit political, cultural, and social influences upon these types of spaces; it asks if spatial agency can be located and if yes, where, and how architectural thinking can bring new insight into these subjects. The book is not as much about the practice of architecture but rather, the theories and influences shaping the built environment. The project is both a critique of the discipline and its perceived boundaries and an effort to expand and blur these boundaries so that architecture becomes more engaged in positively affecting the world.

The polarization of reproductive healthcare in North America provides a platform to consider a series of interconnected relationships. These include the precarity of access to reproductive healthcare, the autonomy of a woman's body, state and federal controls that manipulate space, ways in which design thinking can transform spatial relationships, and possibilities for agency to be discovered within these complex issues. The book delves into a series of research areas, two of which include legal rulings that directly define spatial relationships and the examination of some of the most restrictive state legislation at the time of publication.

Buffer Zone Ordinance
The codification of spatial terms through several United States (US) Supreme Court decisions has created legal precedent. I would like to highlight one that initially began in Boulder, Colorado's 1986 City Council that eventually made its way to the Supreme Court in *Hill v Colorado* (2000). Boulder established a 'Buffer Zone Ordinance' to protect those attempting to access reproductive healthcare from the intensity of protestors creating unsafe areas in and around abortion clinics in Boulder. The Buffer Zone Ordinance stipulated that within 100 feet of a clinic or office a demonstrator could not

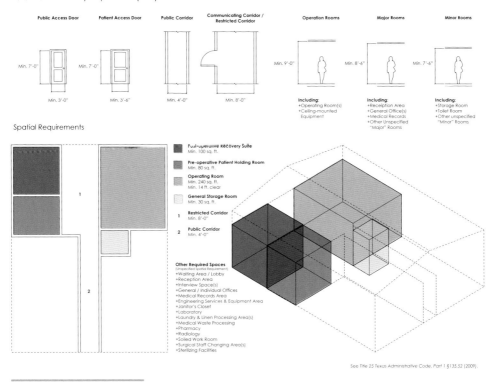

FIGURE 2. Texas Building Code Analysis, 2016. Image courtesy of the author.

approach someone closer than eight feet without explicit permission, creating a bubble of protection around someone entering or exiting a building.[11] Although the First Amendment of the United States Constitution protects freedom of speech and the right of people to peaceably protest and assemble, speech cannot prevent someone from gaining access to an intended space. However, because the Court is so protective of speech—one of the distinguishing legal parameters of the United States—it begs questioning what are the limits of speech? When does the right to physical access become an equal or greater concern than ensuring the right for someone to 'peaceably' assemble and express their point of view? And what does peaceably really mean in this context? Very often these protests are not peaceful, they are anything but. A conflict arises between public safety and free speech. Yes, speech should be unencumbered and yes, a person should be able to freely walk through the front door of an abortion clinic. However, the reality of these situations demonstrates otherwise. The Courts have stated their concern for public safety, for ensuring the safety of abortion procedures, for ensuring a woman's constitutional right to inter-state travel to have an abortion, and that this right should not

be "sacrificed in the interest of a defendants' First Amendment rights."[12] You may vehemently disagree with abortion, but your point of view cannot legally prevent an individual from accessing her right to obtain care. In *Hill v Colorado*, the Supreme Court agreed with the lower court's decision and accepted the protective distances the City Council created—later supported by the State Court. Literal distances became inscribed around bodies and buildings—upheld and thus protected by the Court.

Depending where in the United States a woman lives, she may find abortion access to not be an issue or it may be far more difficult to locate a provider. According to the Guttmacher Institute, over eighty-nine percent of counties in the US lack an abortion provider. During the time period of research for this book, the most restrictive states included South Dakota, North Dakota, Mississippi, Kentucky, Nebraska, and Utah. Although in somewhat constant flux, today this list includes Mississippi, Texas, Virginia, Arkansas, and Alabama. Each state was examined more closely to understand what were the social, politic, and economic factors influencing abortion access.

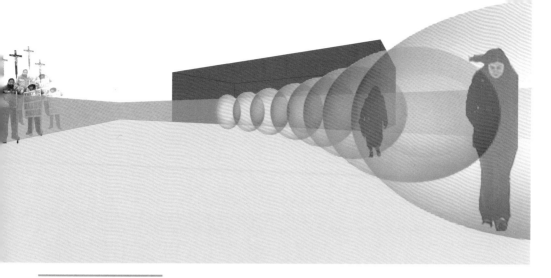

FIGURE 3. Hill v. Colorado in Contested Spaces: Abortion Clinics, Women's Shelters and Hospitals, 2013. Image courtesy of the author.

Mississippi

According to the Gallup Political Poll, Mississippi rates as the "Most Conservative State" in the United States.[13] The state also has the highest rate of teen pregnancy.[14] The Mississippi state government has successfully passed a series of restrictive abortion legislation aimed at making abortion more difficult to access. At the time of the research, some of these laws included twenty-four-hour waiting periods and doctor only requirements for state regulated patient consultations. The doctor-only requirement for the abortion procedure creates a situation where accessing an abortion, although legal on paper, is quite difficult for poor women of color. Because doctors must either fly or drive to the only remaining abortion clinic in Mississippi, scheduling patients for both their counseling and their procedures is a complex and time sensitive process. These inter-related complexities can add expense and time to accessing care. The longer a woman has to wait, the more expensive the procedure becomes if it moves into the second trimester. This results in missing work, needing childcare, and even overnight accommodations if the procedure is scheduled outside of the twenty-four hours since the time of counseling.

Poor women of color are seeking abortion at a greater rate than other women according to the Guttmacher Institute. Poverty rates for Mississippi are above the national average and even more so for female head of household with children under five years of age. At the time of publication, the US federal poverty line for an individual was $8,240, for a family of two was $11,060, and for a family of four was $16,700. For example, individual versus female head of household poverty rates for Jackson were 23.5% to 53.5%, for Biloxi 14.6% to 50.7%, and for Natchez 28.6% to 75.1%.[15] These are significant poverty statistics placing enormous financial difficulties on a woman's ability to afford an abortion.

In order to expand access, one can creatively imagine a few possibilities. One way is to require all hospitals to provide the full spectrum of reproductive healthcare for all women. The state would go from having one clinic to having 112 hospitals providing abortion services—exponentially increasing access across the state. Another way is to ensure that all pharmacies stock and sell emergency contraception (EC). After collecting data determining whether all the pharmacies across the state stocked and sold EC, it became apparent that EC was not readily available to all women. This data is now included in the American Society for Emergency Contraception database—an unexpected connection that has expanded this research beyond the discipline of architecture.

2: Action and Activist Endeavors

My second book has led to various research tangents including design work for several US clinics, abortion clinic building code analyses, serving as an expert witness, and interdisciplinary collaborations that explore reproductive healthcare access—all of which have extended architecture's engagement beyond the discipline.

As a result of visiting many independent providers across the United States, it became apparent that there is a need for design to engage this ignored population. There are many contributions architects can make to reproductive healthcare facilities. In conjunction with ArchiteXX, the New York City women and architecture organization I co-founded, we created a design call for ideas "Private Choices Public Spaces," for the Jackson, Mississippi clinic's public space and entrance zones. To quote directly from our design call:

> Design is a powerful, effective, and often under-utilized tool in addressing the complexities of contested spaces. ArchiteXX calls you to collaborate with us in a practice of active citizenship through design. We believe design must engage challenging social and political dimensions of the built environment, such as access to reproductive health care, in order to make improvements at all scales for all people. The public-private threshold of an abortion clinic is a highly-nuanced interface of strong personal sentiments. Our design action takes the discomfort head-on, illuminating the spatial implications of access to reproductive health care and the role design can play in expanding the conversation.

ArchiteXX initiated this design action to put our values regarding the profession of architecture into practice. The design action promotes dialogue and collaboration rather than competition to execute its goal. Through this mode of activism, we hope to transform the profession.[16]

Birthing, Bodies + Borders
This new body of research examines birthing centers solely dedicated to foreign women seeking to give birth in the United States. Often right across the US–Mexico border, or embedded within residential neighborhoods in Californian cities, these spaces are often but not always hidden, even camouflaged within their built environments. The project intersects with a host of complex issues including birthing and healthcare within both domestic and commercial spaces; how the borders of country and nation state are understood and legally transgressed; and how basic human rights of childbirth and family are represented and manipulated as an act of political will and defiance. The project will explore how space participates in these debates, how legal definitions of the body, borders, national identities, and citizenship are understood theoretically, spatially, and practiced on-the-ground, and how the rights of these women are either supported or undermined as a result of ongoing political negotiations among various actors and nations involved.

Women in Architecture: ArchiteXX
ArchiteXX is a New York City women and architecture organization whose mission seeks to bridge academy and practice. We create opportunities to raise awareness of women in the discipline both within schools, out in practice, and within the broader public. There are four primary facets to our work: mentoring, writing, advocacy, and action-oriented efforts.

Two programming efforts demonstrate ways we are creating more exposure for women. We are committed to exposing all students to more women architects and designers. Our university hub programming does this. Through collaboration with students and faculty at different schools across New York State, we position more women in the public arena of architecture programs and diversify and expand possibilities for our discipline to engage the world. In organizing a brown-bag lecture series, we want more women to become a part of a school's primary lecture series—a bottom up effort for change. Additionally, we would like to enable students to network with other architecture and design programs beyond their own school in order to expand their professional connections prior to graduation.

The second effort is our ongoing wikiD project. We are deconstructing the architectural canon by writing more women into Wikipedia. The initial idea emerged after reading Despina Stratigakos's *Places* essay, "Unforgetting Women Architects:

From the Pritzker to Wikipedia" where she discusses women being literally edited out of Wikipedia.[17] Her essay inspired me to take action to reverse this trend and write a new history where women are included in our history. WikiD is now in its third year. Until there is gender parity on Wikipedia, we will continue to write more women in.

The last item here discussed is a new project with Karen Burns, *The Bloomsbury Global Encyclopedia of Women in Architecture, 1960–2015*. This will be the first ever English language global compendium that solely examines women working within the built environment. Although close to half of all architecture students in many countries across the world are women, there remains a dearth of scholarship about women at a global scale. The book is critical in providing a wider and more inclusive array of architectural examples to better educate all students and the general public about the role women contribute to our built world. This book will not mirror the male canon of architecture but rather, put forward a more diverse, even radical idea, of how architecture is practiced by women. We will focus on a wide array of subjects. These will include the known women designers, under-recognized women practitioners, under-represented communities who have demonstrated a transformative effect at local or national scales, architectural critics, and theorists who have pioneered discussion of gender, equity, and minorities, thus diversifying the discipline. It will also feature significant women educators and influential architecture schools establishing new pedagogy, curriculum, and discourse, women working in government architecture and public works departments, as well as international policy and professional endeavors.

What I seek is not only disruption of the status quo, but also complete reconfiguration of our discipline: who and how we practice; who, how and what we teach, all in order to broaden engagement with our contemporary conditions.

3: A Few Concluding Thoughts
As Elizabeth Grosz writes:

> How to *think* architecture differently? How to think *in* architecture, or *of* architecture, without conforming to the standard assumptions …[18] [i]nsofar as architecture is seeking not so much 'innovation,' not simply 'the latest fad,' but to produce differently, to engender the new … How to keep architecture open to its outside, how to force architecture to *think*?[19]

I, too, want architecture to be more and do more than it currently is doing. This requires an expansion of how we teach and think about the discipline and our ethical responsibilities to the built environment. My work can be located within what is described as action-based design research. Research that leads to action. For me, this includes affecting power relations within the academy and the discipline's perceived boundaries of architectural engagement in the world. The various facets of my research work to build a different, more engaged, and expansive discipline—both in the academy and out in the world. This requires that:

1.   ARCHITECTURE MUST POLITICALLY PARTICIPATE TO BE VITAL

and that we,

2.   DO ARCHITECTURE DIFFERENTLY

As long as there are opportunities for architectural involvement, I am compelled to engage, take action, and help foster agency. I believe it speaks to what Patricia Maguire writes is a broader "commitment to a liberatory, transformational project that is essential to any definition of feminism and feminist scholarship."[20]

3.   ACT

According to Maguire, "At its core, feminism and its scholarship is a political movement for social, structural, and personal transformation."[21] As she cites Liz Stanley, "the point is to challenge the world, not only study it."[22] Or in architecture's case, not only design it.

Endnotes

1. "status quo, n." *OED Online*. March 2019. Oxford University Press. http://www.oed.com.libezproxy2.syr.edu/view/Entry/189357?redirectedFrom=status+quo.

2. Educational enrollments begin the transformation of the numbers in the disciplines. For more on the numbers of women in these fields, see: "More Women Than Men Enrolled in U.S. Medical Schools in 2017," *Association of American Medical Colleges*, Monday, December 18, 2017, https://news.aamc.org/press-releases/article/applicant-enrollment-2017/; Elizabeth Olson, "Women Make Up Majority of U.S. Law Students for the First Time," *The New York Times*, December 16, 2016, https://www.nytimes.com/2016/12/16/business/dealbook/women-majority-of-us-law-students-first-time.html; "Quick Take: Women in Male-Dominated Industries and Occupations," *Catalyst*, August 23, 2018, https://www.catalyst.org/research/women-in-male-dominated-industries-and-occupations/; Despina Stratigakos, "Why is the world of architecture so male-dominated?" *Los Angeles Times*, April 21, 2016, https://www.latimes.com/opinion/op-ed/la-oe-stratigakos-missing-women-architects-20160421-story.html; "Professional Active Physicians by Gender," *Kaiser Family Foundation*, March 2019, https://www.kff.org/other/state-indicator/physicians-by-gender/?dataView=1&currentTimeframe=0&sortModel=%7B%22colId%22:%22Location%22,%22sort%22:%22asc%22%7D; Jennifer Cheeseman Day, "More Than 1 in 3 Lawyers are Women," *United States Census Bureau*, May 8, 2018, https://www.census.gov/library/stories/2018/05/women-lawyers.html.

3. Lori Brown, *Feminist Practices: Interdisciplinary Approaches to Women and Architecture* (Surrey, England: Ashgate Publishing Limited, 2011), Introduction and Conclusion.

4. Nancy Duncan, *Bodyspace: Destablizing Geographies of Gender and Sexuality* (London: Routledge, 1996), 245, 247.

5. Linda McDowell, *Gender, Identity and Place* (Minneapolis: University of Minnesota Press, 1999), 7–8.

6. Feminist Pedagogy Working Group, "Defining Feminism," in *Feminist Geography in Practice Research and Methods*, ed. Pamela Moss (Oxford: Blackwell Publishers Ltd, 2002), 22.

7. Ibid.

8. Kimberle Crenshaw, "Mapping the Margins: Intersectionality, Identity Politics, and Violence against Women of Color," *Stanford Law Review* 43, no. 6 (July 1991): 1,244.

9. Ibid., 1,244-45, footnote 9.

10. "Interview with Angela Davis by Southbank Centre's Artistic Director Jude Kelly for Women on the World series," March 11, 2017. https://www.youtube.com/watch?v=lBgdzK3jfEg&feature=youtu.be.

11. Dr. Warren M. Hern, "Abortion 'bubble bill' going before U.S. Supreme Court," June 11, 2000, http://www.drhern.com/bubblelaw.htm.

12. Schenck v. Pro Choice Network of Western New York (1997).

13. Jeffrey M. Jones, "Mississippi Rates as the Most Conservative U.S. State," *GALLUP Politics*, February 25, 2011, http://www.gallup.com/poll/146348/mississippi-rates-conservative-state.aspx/.

14. Brady E. Hamilton and Stephanie J. Ventura, "Birth Rates for U.S. Teenagers Reach Historic Lows for All Age and Ethnic Groups," *NCHS Data Brief*, No. 89, April 2012.

15. Lori A. Brown, *Contested Spaces: Abortion Clinics, Women's Shelters and Hospitals* (Surrey: England, Ashgate Publishing Limited, 2013), Chapter 5.

16. "Private Choices Public Spaces 2014 Design Action," *ArchiteXX*, accessed March 21, 2019, https://www.architexx.org/action/design-action/pcps.

17. Despina Stratigakos, "Unforgetting Women Architects: From the Pritzker to Wikipedia," *Places Journal*, (April 2016): https://doi.org/10.22269/130603.

18. Elizabeth Grosz, *Architecture from the Outside Essays on Virtual and Real Space* (Massachusetts: MIT Press, 2001), 59.

19. Ibid., 64.

20. Patricia Maguire, "Uneven Ground: Feminisms and Action Research," in *Handbook of Action Research*, ed. Peter Reason and Hilary Bradbury (London: Sage Publications, 2006), 61.

21. Ibid.

22. Ibid.

IN DEFENSE OF NEW YORK'S LOFT LAW

AFFORDABLE HOUSING FOR ALL

Julie Torres Moskovitz

Fete Nature Architecture (FNA) is an upstander architecture firm. Upstander is defined as someone who sees wrong and acts. Lately, we have had the sense that this is 'our time' to do something about social justice, gender equality, and climate change. The first steps are via collective participation in social dialogue, and via discomfort and challenge we learn about new viewpoints that need to be considered. Listening to and synthesizing the needs of the community—this form of engagement is critical to the outcomes of programming and design. FNA's research and design work have taken us to every borough of New York City (NYC). Being active and engaged has led to an architecture practice that is more in touch with the city, its strengths, and its weaknesses.

FNA studio is a vital, collaborative firm whose process is founded in investigations of new ways to inhabit the urban fabric. This method of working is informed by an aptitude for green technologies, resiliency, materiality, and unique fabrication methods. FNA studio's architecture is whimsical while being grounded in our belief that architecture must be proactive to improve upon societal norms. FNA is adaptable, optimistic, and rigorous in all of its undertakings. FNA studio works on projects as wide-ranging as collaborations with artists and actors, passive house buildings, Build-

it-Back resilient homes for recovery from Hurricane Sandy, and visualizations of exemplary spaces and places for communities, nonprofits, and institutions. The Loft Law project is an important aspect of FNA's portfolio of civically minded projects.

In fall 2016, the Ghost Ship Warehouse burned to the ground in Oakland, California, killing thirty-six inhabitants—musicians, artists, students—who comprised a community of creative tenants working and living in a factory building that was not zoned for residential use. As it exists in NYC, these tenants in Oakland did not have a legal pathway for bringing their building up to code. After the fire, officials from Oakland attended a NYC Department of Cultural Affairs and Loft Board-sponsored meeting with artists and Loft Law tenants to learn more about Loft Law and how it works.[1]

In essence, NYC Loft Law is a role model for other American cities facing similar issues with commercial and industrial buildings that landlords rent to residential tenants. A recent University of California, Berkeley, city planning studio researched cities around the country including San Francisco, Baltimore, Denver, Minneapolis, and Seattle for examples of how city agencies set policies to deal with live/work tenants occupying warehouse buildings.[2] In New York City, Loft Law is a daringly clever way to problem-solve with multiple stakeholders—including building owners and renters. It establishes a pathway to legality and safety. The New York State Multiple Dwelling Law gives authority to NYC, via Executive Order No. 66 dated September 30, 1982, to establish the New York City Loft Board. The Loft Board regulates the legal conversion of certain lofts from commercial/manufacturing to safe code-compliant residential use. This model seeks to bring buildings up to code, increase safety for residential inhabitants, and legalize a building with economic viability in mind. This is all accomplished with residential tenants remaining in place for a win-win scenario. Under this model, the landlord achieves a residential Certificate of Occupancy, while tenants obtain rent stabilization.

As many urban neighborhoods throughout the United States face extreme pressures of gentrification and densification, it is important to recognize the value of Loft Law for tenants, landlords, and the city as a whole.

Today, NYC is experiencing a housing crisis, with the majority of city residents being rent-burdened: more than thirty percent of their income is used to pay rent.[3] Michael Greenberg wrote, in "Tenants Under Siege: Inside New York City's Housing Crisis" that:

> New York City is in the throes of a humanitarian emergency … New York is what aid groups would characterize as a complex emergency: man-made and shaped by a combination of forces that have led to a large-scale displacement of populations from their homes.[4]

It may be surprising, but:

> rent-stabilized apartments are disappearing at an alarming rate: since 2007, at least 172,000 apartments have been deregulated. To give an example of how quickly affordable housing can vanish, between 2007 and 2014, twenty-five percent of the rent-stabilized apartments on the Upper West Side of Manhattan were deregulated.[5]

The conversion of existing warehouses to residential use is one way of warding off these pressures. A corollary benefit is that Loft Law buildings highlight the industrial heritage of the area. The physical buildings are saved from demolition, which provides historical context, including brick and mortar, well-proportioned volumes, arched windows, and factory signage in quickly morphing neighborhoods of new condominiums. What would SoHo be without its commercial and manufacturing cast iron buildings?

FIGURE 1. Mapping of Loft Law Buildings in NYC. Blue pins represent buildings designated Loft Law Buildings in 1982 and 1987 under Multiple Dwelling Law Article C (281(1) and (281(4)), while Orange Pins represent building that qualified for Loft Law coverage under the 2010 law (MDL Article C 281(5)). Image courtesy of Fete Nature Architecture.

FIGURE 2. Images from Loft Law Interim Multiple Dwelling Units (IMDs) featuring the architecture of converted manufacturing buildings to accommodate Live/Work needs for tenants that include artists, architects, chefs, writers, musicians, dancers, teachers, tech workers, small business owners, etc. Note that names were changed here to protect tenants. Photography courtesy of Fete Nature Architecture.

Williamsburg, Brooklyn, without its industrial warehouses, becomes a blank canvas for generic residential condominium buildings and box stores. New buildings can add interest to the skyline, but wholesale new neighborhoods neuter the history and cultural resources of that area. This is not an exaggeration, as driving through swathes of Greenpoint, Williamsburg, Bushwick, Gowanus, Long Island City, and Mott Haven will reveal a 360-degree view of all new residential towers and mid-rise condominiums, with empty billiard tables and libraries as first-floor amenities. Driving down Kent Avenue along the East River proves that very few industrial buildings survived the speculative market pressures resulting from the 2005 rezoning of Williamsburg. And it should be noted, some of the most compelling industrial buildings which have been repurposed, are Loft Law buildings.

In defense of Loft Law, it is important to dispel myths perpetuated by city planners, architects, lawyers, and others who don't have a good grasp of the intricacies of the law, yet share misinformation. There are many misconceptions as far as Loft Law tenants and buildings go. Here are a few:

They are squatters. Loft Law tenants pay rent. Tenants in buildings covered by the 2010 Loft Law pay slightly below-market-rate rent, but this is justified considering that their buildings are run-down, with leaky roofs, outdated appliances and electrical fixtures, drafty building envelopes, and inadequate heat, while also lacking a superintendent, doormen, and amenities like laundry rooms, communal roof decks, etc.

They are gentrifiers causing gentrification. This is not true. Most buildings with Loft Law tenants were previously empty having long seen the end of industrial manufacturing, inhabited with artists and others who dared to live in run-down buildings in order to have space for working and living. Although each new wave that moves into a neighborhood may contribute indirectly to an increase in rent, in the cost of food, and in the number of coffee shops, factors such as new public transportation lines, rezoning, and government incentives contribute much more towards gentrification.

Loft Law Tenants don't deserve to be rent-stabilized because others with more financial need should have priority. All people at all income levels deserve to live and thrive in NYC. As Mayor de Blasio's re-election campaign slogan claimed, "This is Your City." Many different types of families and persons live in a Loft Law building: many of the inhabitants, at lower- and middle-income levels, live paycheck-to-paycheck and are rent-burdened.[6] Students who often owe upwards of $100,000 in student loan debt have a right to make a go of roommate-style living in NYC as they begin their careers. Small businesses often start in a loft space where live/work is permitted and small businesses help to create self-sufficiency and job growth. Loft Law tenants also advocate for affordable housing, retaining rent-stabilized units, and increasing affordability opportunities in this ever more expensive city.

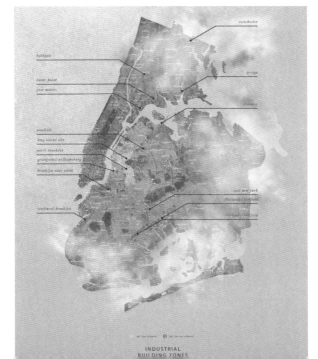

FIGURE 3. Map of NYC Loft Law Buildings highlighted as pins in red or yellow. Industrial Business Zones (IBZs) highlighted in red protect manufacturing and do not permit a Loft Law building. Three exceptions, highlighted in yellow, are permitted to contain Loft Law buildings within the IBZs. TWilliamsburg, Greenpoint, and Long Island City have experienced displacement of both residential and light industrial manufacturing tenants during the 2005 Williamsburg rezoning. Image courtesy of Fete Nature Architecture.

They shouldn't have rented in a commercial building. Many of the industrial buildings with residential tenants were presented to potential renters as just that—residential rental apartments. Real estate agents have shown and listed these spaces as apartment units. People moving into an apartment building often don't know how to check the status of the Certificate of Occupancy on the NYC Department of Building website. Furthermore, they don't even suspect that they should check after they attend an open-house for an apartment in a building that is filled with residential apartments.

The landlord should be able to make decisions about their own building and hence should be free to evict tenants. It is true that landlords of private property are entitled to invest money into their buildings and to modify them as they see fit, as long as these modifications meet the Authority Having Jurisdiction's requirements. Without exception, these industrial buildings have Certificate of Occupancies for manufacturing or commercial use and landlords rented them out as residential apartments. This is unlawful and dangerous. In many cases the landlords collected money from those tenants over decades and allowed tenants to make physical modifications and improvements to buildings. The Loft Law Interim Multiple Dwellings (IMD) status puts the building on the pathway to a residential Certificate of Occupancy which benefits both the landlords and the tenants. The landlords are on a legalization pathway that brings the building up to code compliance for a residential Certificate of Occupancy while avoiding displacement of tenants. This creates safe living conditions and a safe city. The landlord has avenues to seek eviction if tenants are not complying with access or payment under certain conditions, via the Housing Court.

Bankers live in these Loft Law buildings, not artists. While there may be a few wealthy bankers living in Loft Law apartments, the vast majority of tenants are not. One example Loft Law building in Williamsburg has tenants who work in creative fields such as; art, acting, architecture, music, graphic design, cooking, filmset-styling, teaching, and writing. Students and many children live in these buildings as well.

Now that we have addressed misinformation and rumors, let's look at how Loft Law came about. It dates back to SoHo artist tenant activism of the 1970s, when fabricators moved out of commercial and manufacturing spaces in Manhattan, leaving landlords in need of rent income. Artists moved in and physically worked on their spaces, adding plumbing fixtures, electricity, and other improvements. They paid rent in order to live in high-ceilinged, open spaces where they could create their art. This enabled a whole community of artists to establish themselves in SoHo, NoHo, and TriBeCa, and today a number of these artists, including Donald Judd, Andy Warhol, Jean-Michel Basquiat, Philip Glass, Eva Hesse, and Twyla Tharp, are world-renowned. Here is an excerpt directly from the Loft Law Board's website:

FIGURE 4. Axonometric drawing of a Loft Law building (29,000 sq.ft. warehouse) in Brooklyn that includes residential and live/work tenant spaces. Highlighted are IMD units where eleven tenants were interviewed. Image courtesy of Fete Nature Architecture.

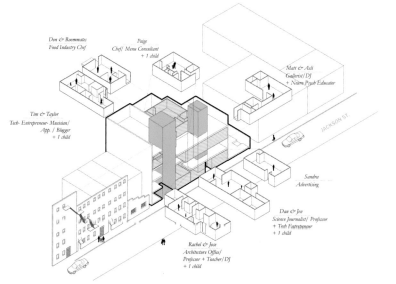

In 1982, the New York State Legislature enacted the New York City Loft Law and established the New York City Loft Board to regulate the legal conversion of certain lofts in the city from commercial/manufacturing use to residential use. Article 7-C of the Multiple Dwelling Law (MDL), also known as the Loft Law, created a new classification of buildings in New York City known as interim multiple dwellings (IMD). Generally, this classification encompasses formally commercial and manufacturing loft spaces that were used as residences by at least three independent families during the period of April 1, 1980 through December 1, 1981. Because these lofts failed to meet the fire safety and other code requirements for legal residential occupancy, the Loft Law also established the Loft Board with the mission of coordinating the legal conversion of these spaces to safe residential use.[7]

Subsequently, in June 2010, after much tenant advocacy in Albany:

the New York State Legislature amended the Loft Law to include units in a commercial or manufacturing building where three or more families have lived independently from one another for twelve consecutive months from January, 2008 through December, 2009, in a building that lacks a residential certificate of occupancy.[8]

FIGURE 5. Screening and talk with a film director for *no-wave* films held within a Loft Law residential unit that operated an artist collective called "Louis V ESP." Photography by Ethan Miller.

FIGURE 6. Images from Loft Law Apartments featuring aspects of converted manufacturing buildings to accommodate live/work needs. Depicted here from left to right is an image of an entry, cooking equipment storage, an art installation, and a small mezzanine accessed by a ladder on castors. Names were changed here to protect tenants. Photography courtesy of Fete Nature Architecture.

  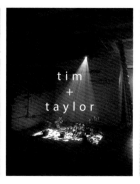 

The 1982 and 2010 Loft Laws granted eligible tenants an important pathway to live in safe buildings, while vanquishing fears of displacement or eviction. Our 2016 mapping of Loft Law buildings, listed in the Loft Law Board Meeting Minutes and found in archival data, allowed us to identify 973 buildings—773 of which were from the original 1982 Loft Law and another 200 buildings from the newer 2010 Loft Law.[9] Approximately 100 more buildings applied for Loft Law status after our mapping and prior to the end of the Loft Law protection bill on June 15, 2017. Even though there are fewer 2010 Loft Law buildings, it is important to note that, in general, the 2010 buildings are larger and hence, house many more Loft Law tenants.[10]

Where are we today? NYC Loft Tenant (NYCLT) activists traveled to the New York state capital in Albany to attend 2017 and 2018 Sessions and to meet with Senate and Assembly members who co-sponsored a bill to extend the current 2010 Loft Law application period, and to eliminate previous exclusions—the "Bloomberg Exclusions."[11] The bill was not passed in the Senate for two years. Once again, in spring 2019, a bill has been sponsored in the Assembly and Senate called the Loft Law Clean-Up Bill which may pass before the Session ends in June. Both pro-tenant and pro-landlord efforts in Albany are underway. Currently no method to achieve the NYC Loft Law pathway—an otherwise exemplary model studied by other cities—exists since the expiration of Loft Law in summer 2017. There are approximately 395 buildings still under consideration for Loft Law Board jurisdiction. Such protections are available only to those who applied prior to June 15, 2017—an unfortunate situation as many more 'illegal' buildings or units with IMD status could be placed on a pathway for life safety and code compliance.

The "Narrative Statement Process," established by the Loft Law Board, is a unique method for tenants to work collaboratively with their landlords on their loft interiors toward the goal of legalization. The "Narrative Statement" is a detailed description in plain language of landlord work proposed for each unit and common areas. It accompanies the building owner's drawings and specification proposal. Distinctive to the process, are a series of informal meetings in which tenants and landlords negotiate and agree on interior unit plans and public common areas in the presence of Loft Law staff. This serves as a vital tool for tenants to be able to participate in the design process with their architect and have input on their live/work space. The owner files for NYC Department of Building approvals and as the owner learns of objections from the Department of Buildings, the tenants and their architect are given an opportunity to weigh in on code-compliant counter-proposals for interior partitions and habitable room types that could exist within an apartment. It is feasible, for instance that a landlord may want to tear down all interior walls, which would eliminate the possibility of private bedrooms and sleeping alcoves, otherwise needed by families and roommates. The "Narrative Statement Process" provides a voice for stakeholders to work together and agree to a plan to amend the filing set for submission to the NYC Department of Buildings. There are shared costs, which are frequently spread over a period of ten years or more. Meanwhile, tenant apartments are subject to regulated rent increases as their landlord meets benchmarks in the "Narrative Statement Process." Over time, the Loft Law building moves from an industrial building, to an Interim Multiple Dwelling, to a legal residential building with a final Certificate of Occupancy, at which point the tenants will have rent stabilization.

How do we make this somewhat obscure and little understood policy public? Many eligible residents in illegal buildings are not aware of Loft Law. The City Planning Department and other city agencies do not appear to have adequate funding to publicize it, nor do they have much incentive to promote converting occupied warehouses to Loft Law buildings when private development real estate deals make the city glitter and shine. To further complicate matters, there are many different advocates and non-profits for other constituents in need, who feel that Loft Law tenants are less deserving of advocacy. Why should Loft Law tenants have a pathway with so many other needier constituents? However, this sort of 'scarcity mindset,' which has a narrow group determining which segments of the population will receive a pathway to opportunity, will leave many out of the equation. Instead, we are better off recognizing that the majority of our NYC renters live rent-burdened and are fearful of displacement or eviction. There is a need for affordable live/work units. Live/work has enabled me to raise a family while also running my own architecture firm from out of my apartment and for my husband to teach English at a NYC public school. More strategies, incentives, and pathways are needed to help alleviate this crisis at low income and middle-income levels, as wealthier developers have tax abatements and subsidies to benefit them. Students burdened by thousands of dollars in debt deserve a chance to live in a lower rent space while contributing to society and starting their careers. Families deserve a chance to stay in the city to raise their children instead of moving farther out and commuting back into the city for work. Small business entrepreneurs deserve a chance to get off the ground in a combined live/work space. Loft Law is one such pathway and it is an exemplary model for other cities concerned with life safety and the displacement of populations.

To this end, we need large, out-of-the-box thinking to address climate change, resiliency, and the housing crisis.

As pilot projects for the introduction of large-scale renewable technologies on their roofs, these live/work buildings could establish the twenty-first-century model of housing for young families. Projects like these could not only provide creative and entrepreneurial jobs for NYC residents, but they could also provide energy. The twenty-four/seven communities in these Loft Law buildings, dispersed throughout the five boroughs, could establish live/work nodes as networked eco-systems serving as resilient community hubs and micro-energy providers for their respective neighborhoods. Currently, these industrial buildings blend in, but the more the city tears down and builds new, the rarer these industrial relics will become. Our interviews with tenants in three case study buildings provide a cross-section of the creative types living here, from artists to musicians, to food and tech industry workers, to teachers and professors. All share the ability to career shift and adjust to economic pressures of living/working in NYC, which oftentimes means balancing three or four jobs at the same time.

These buildings contain communities that offer services to their neighborhoods while their building façades provide a history that matters to each block. The city can change the public's perception of these buildings as squatter buildings (a false idea that is a remnant from the eighties) and promote the notion that these buildings house thriving, creative communities and are green-tech retrofitted treasures that add character to the city. These buildings can become exemplary green buildings, which could serve as micro-energy hubs and as incubators or creative business centers. Loft Law tenants fortify the community, as the hard-working factory laborers who worked in these buildings once did. And Loft Law buildings are allies of light industry and manufacturing buildings and should work to protect them in neighboring Industrial Business Zones.

NYC must also be resilient, as we have learned from Hurricane Sandy recovery work and the Build-It-Back program—projects which I participated in while redesigning several damaged homes in the Canarsie section of Brooklyn. This experience has taught me that the idea of a micro-grid and local neighborhood power hub on the roof of a Loft Law Building with a large footprint, is not far-fetched. The Power Rockaways Resilience plan, developed by Coastal Marine Resource Center (CMRC) with a grant from NYCEDC, has small businesses equipped with solar-powered generators, geo-thermal heating, and resilient measures to serve as a hub for the Rockaways community in the event of future disasters. This would ensure that

FIGURE 7. LEIMAY studio at CAVE in the Williamsburg Section of Brooklyn: for over twenty years, home of multidisciplinary artists Ximena Garnica, Shige Moriya, and their collaborators. The studio is part of a live/work space in a building applying for NYC Loft Law coverage. Photography by Ximena Garnica.

no Rockaways citizen is more than a ten-minute walk from a business with off-grid energy.[12] CMRC has currently translated this model for scaled-up replication in Puerto Rico, currently recovering from Hurricane Maria. The loss of power Puerto Rico experienced was as debilitating for hospitals, communities, and local businesses as it was for the Rockaways and other neighborhoods following Hurricane Sandy. To plan for the future of our city, we must overlap safety nets for tenant safety, resiliency, and for energy-efficiency

How does Fete Nature Architecture's interest in Loft Law fit into our architecture practice? It helps keep us informed on tenant/landlord struggles and answers questions about live/work identities in the twenty-first century. What can I do as an architect and as a citizen who cares about equity for all and about problem-solving at the policy and city level?

Architects can have a role in policy-making and in understanding all sides, advocating for the best approach to resolve the problems while creating a safer city.

While architects are always designing for clients, they may not always take the time to study what the positive and negative impacts of their designs mean for a community. As of May 2018, I've held a mayoral-appointed position as a public Loft Law board member charged with participating in the process of legislative rule-making and public hearings with an aim to make policy more public.

Acknowledgments
This paper was originally published as part of an editorial piece entitled, "In Defense of Loft Law," written by Julie Torres Moskovitz, a loft law tenant and architect. The larger piece synthesized research and tenant interviews conducted by Team AJX (Angela Co, Julie Torres Moskovitz, Xiaoyin Li. Support Team: Daniel Asoli, Meghan Grimes, Thomas Kuei, and Geraldine Vargas). Part I of the research analyzed patterns of rent-stabilized Loft Law buildings and Interim Multiple Dwellings (IMDs) through: opportunity/threat mapping; interviews with tenants and professionals working with the Loft Law Board; analysis of policy and regulations; and drawings studies of existing conditions and layouts of several case study Loft Law units. Part II of the on-going research includes schematic design of speculative live/work models of zero-energy solutions that incorporate solar panels on their expansive roofs and that promote neighborhood-based creative centers that share resiliency with the community.

The research was made possible by the Summer 2016 Fellows Program at the Institute for Public Architecture, which answered a call for how to create affordable live/work in NYC, per Mayor de Blasio's ONE NYC plan.[13]

Endnotes

1   Leaders of NYC Loft Law Tenants Group presented this information in a public meeting on June 2, 2017. Participating were the NYC Department of Cultural Affairs and Loft Board (with Executive Director Helaine Balsa) and this included a presentation on Loft Law with Ron Vidal who is on the leadership and strategy steering committee of WABA (We the Artists of The Bay Area) and a professional in fire management as well as a volunteer firefighter. See "City Reminds New Yorkers of Upcoming Deadline to Apply for Loft Law protection Under NY State Law," City of New York, April 27, 2017, accessed March 19, 2019, http://www1.nyc.gov/site/buildings/about/pr-loft-law.page.

2   Viktor Bensus, Irene Calimlin, Anna Cash, Scott Chilberg, Reshad Hai, Eli Kaplan, and Aline Tanielian, *Punitive to Rehabilitative: Strategies for Live-Work Preservation in Oakland* (Oakland, CA: University of California, Berkeley, 2018), https://www.urbandisplacement.org/sites/default/files/images/livework_ucb_studio_report_final.pdf.

3   Michael Greenberg, "Tenants Under Siege: Inside New York City's Housing Crisis," *The New York Review of Books*, August 17, 2017, 75-81.

4   Ibid.

5   Ibid.

6   Viktor Bensus, Irene Calimlin, Anna Cash, Scott Chilberg, Reshad Hai, Eli Kaplan, and Aline Tanielian, *Punitive to Rehabilitative: Strategies for Live-Work Preservation in Oakland*, 43

7   "Welcome to the Loft Board," New York City Loft Board, accessed March 19, 2019, http://www.nyc.gov/html/loft/html/home/home.shtml.

8   There are additional buildings to be added to the 2010 Loft Law building list as our mapping data stopped in August 2016 but the Loft Law was open for applicants until June 2017.

9   "A statement in support of rent-stabilized live/work housing S-0055 and expanding the 2010 Loft Law," NYCLT, Lower Manhattan Loft Tenants, and DUMBO Neighborhood Alliance, April 12, 2015, 2,5.

10 Ibid.

11 Jamie Peck, "New York's Loft Law Is In Danger, A Precious Means of Creating Affordable Housing May be Loft," *Village Voice*, May 25, 2017, accessed March 19, 2019, https://www.villagevoice.com/2017/05/25/nycs-loft-law-is-in-danger.

12 New York Center for Economic Transformation, "Rising to the Challenge Home Free," *NYCEDC* (blog), July 9, 2015, https://www.nycedc.com/blog-entry/rising-challenge-home-free.

13 *One New York The Plan for a Strong and Just City*, The City of New York Mayor Bill de Blasio, 2013, http://www.nyc.gov/html/onenyc/downloads/pdf/publications/OneNYC.pdf.

EQxD FINDINGS FOR AIA:

EQUITY AS A NEW PARADIGM FOR DESIGN PRACTICE

Annelise Pitts

Sometimes, a simple question can spark a movement.

In the summer of 2013, a group of architectural practitioners and affiliated professionals in San Francisco formed Equity by Design (EQxD), a committee of the American Institute of Architects San Francisco (AIASF), to address the following question:

Where are the women architects?

The question, of course, wasn't new. AIA San Francisco's Communications Committee had led sold-out symposia on the topic in 2011 and 2013. Local Women in Architecture committees around the country and throughout the world had been advocating for gender equality in the profession for years. In academia, conferences and symposia had been held, and books had been published on the subject. A widely-publicized petition was circulating to advocate for retroactively awarding the Pritzker Prize to Denise Scott Brown in recognition of her co-authorship

of the work for which her partner, Robert Venturi, had been recognized. Outside of architecture, Sheryl Sandberg and Anne Marie Slaughter had sparked a national conversation about the challenges that working women faced, and on how each of us— individuals, employers, and policy-makers—might take action to promote more healthy and sustainable relationships between our professional and personal lives.

The new AIASF committee decided to build upon this work in several important ways. First, Equity by Design began with the idea that all practitioners, regardless of personal identity, deserved the opportunity to have a sustainable and satisfying career in architecture. The challenges that women faced in the profession, the group believed, were symptomatic of a deeper lack of access to the resources and opportunities that each practitioner and each architectural practice needed in order to thrive. Rather than advocate for women's equal participation in a field that wasn't serving anyone particularly well, Equity by Design set out to change the profession to better serve professionals from all walks of life.

To build this kind of movement, the group needed to understand the broad challenges that the profession faced, as well as the ways in which these dynamics were shaped by their intersections with issues of personal identity. This conversation required the full participation of a diverse range of voices, including those of all genders, races, ethnicities, and cultural backgrounds.

An informed conversation also required new metrics to support the anecdotal evidence that had driven the group to action. This data would be gathered both to demonstrate the scope of the problem at hand and to identify equitable practices that could be implemented by individuals and firm leaders to promote sustainable and satisfying careers in architecture for all individuals.

New questions were born: Why do so many talented young professionals leave the field after practicing for only a few years? Are there specific pinch points that hinder careers in architecture, and do they disproportionately impact women and people of color? How have practitioners managed to work through or around these pinch points? Why did they choose to stay in the field? What makes a career in architecture meaningful and rewarding? Does the burgeoning equity in architecture movement have the opportunity to fundamentally change architectural practice for everyone? The Equity in Architecture Research Project—a multi-phase research initiative—was born to address these issues.

Five years, three national surveys of architecture school graduates, and three sold-out symposia later, Equity by Design has become an integral part of an international movement that seeks to change the way that we practice architecture and interface with our clients, communities, and the built environment. Based on findings from the 2014 survey—where it was noted that the primary reasons that practitioners leave the field are low pay, long hours, and limited advancement opportunities—the following findings from the 2016 survey address the original questions "Where are the women architects?" and "Why do women leave architectural practice?" They also suggest equity-based strategies for moving forward as a profession and respond to our collective call to action by asking: "How can we work together as a professional community to provide all practitioners with access to the resources and opportunities that they need to thrive?"

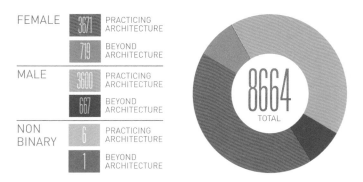

FIGURE 1. Number of Survey Respondents.

Conducted in partnership with the Association of Collegiate Schools of Architecture (ACSA) in March of 2016, the second iteration of the Equity in Architecture survey comprised 124 questions on the education, career experiences, perceptions, and ambitions of graduates of architecture programs in the United States. The survey garnered 8,664 responses, making it the largest survey ever conducted on the topic of equity in architecture in the United States. The study took multiple points into consideration including gender, race, ethnicity, and sexuality. The respondent pool was roughly equally divided between male and female respondents, and also included a small number of non-binary gender respondents.

The resulting analysis presents two closely related frameworks for understanding how issues of equity impact the lives of architecture school graduates. 'Career Dynamics' explores the underlying tensions that persist throughout architecture graduates' professional lives, and the factors that drive career perceptions. Career Pinch Points offers insight into personal and professional milestones that can hinder career progression and influence decisions to leave the field. Several of these topics, including 'Pay Equity,' 'Work-Life Flexibility,' and 'The Glass Ceiling' directly address the most common reasons that practitioners leave the field. In addition, 'Finding the Right Fit' addresses the reasons that practitioners decide to join firms and the factors that make them choose to stay long-term.

FIGURE 2. Life of an Architect.

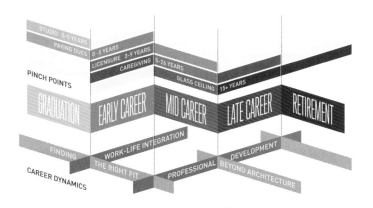

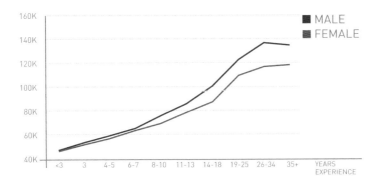

FIGURE 3. Average Salary by Years of Experience.

In both the 2014 and 2016 surveys, one of biggest reasons that respondents—both those who left positions for another position in architecture and those who left the field entirely—cited for leaving their last job in architecture was "low pay." Findings from the 2016 survey indicate that within the profession, average pay is relatively low overall—but especially low for women. At every level of experience, male respondents made more, on average, than their female counterparts—with the largest differences amongst those with the most experience.

A potential explanation for this is the very different roles that mothers and fathers within the sample reported taking in their children's upbringing. Mothers were almost ten times as likely as fathers to report being their children's primary caregiver. In order to better support working mothers, the architectural profession and society at large need to take steps to encourage the equitable distribution of parenting responsibility.

FIGURE 4. Childcare Responsibilities by Gender.

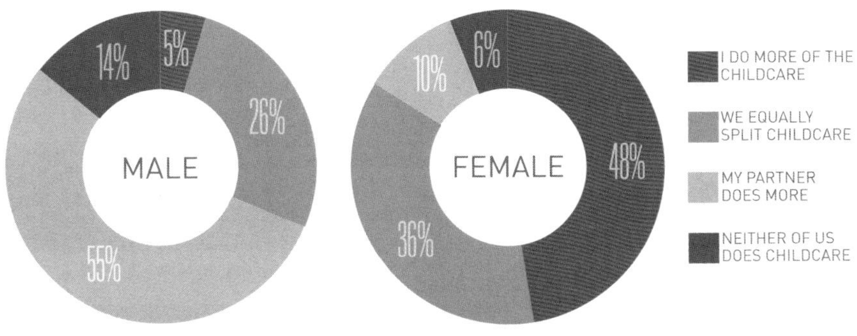

MALE

14% 5%
26%
55%

FEMALE

10% 6%
48%
36%

■ I DO MORE OF THE CHILDCARE

■ WE EQUALLY SPLIT CHILDCARE

■ MY PARTNER DOES MORE

■ NEITHER OF US DOES CHILDCARE

The final predictor of why someone might leave a firm was "lack of advancement opportunity." The 2016 Equity in Architecture survey shows that there is a glass ceiling in architecture that must be addressed. While only eight percent of female respondents and five percent of male respondents reported working in a firm that was mostly or completely led by women, the majority of respondents—male and female—reported working in a firm that was mostly or completely led by men.

FIGURE 5. Gender Balance Among Firm Leadership.

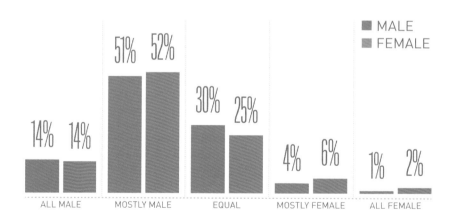

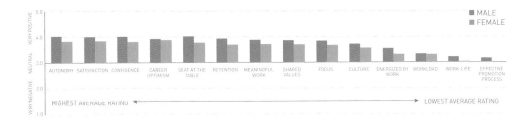

FIGURE 6. Finding the Right Fit: Metrics of Success

When asked about the relative positivity or negativity with which they perceived their careers across fourteen categories, respondents agreed they were mostly satisfied with their level of autonomy, their overall satisfaction, and their confidence in meeting expectations in their current roles. Meanwhile, respondents' perceptions of their firms' promotion processes, their work-life flexibility, and their workloads tended to be least positive. Male respondents' average perceptions were more positive than female respondents' perceptions in each of the fourteen categories, indicating that male practitioners tend to be more holistically satisfied in their careers than female practitioners. Together, these findings suggest that to promote equity in the workplace, firm leaders should aim to address issues with work-life flexibility that are experienced by practitioners of all identities while also making more targeted efforts to close gaps between men's and women's workplace perceptions. These differences in career perceptions are significant because they're deeply intertwined with likelihood of planning to stay in one's current job. The top predictors of planning to stay are: having work that's meaningful and rewarding (results in an eighty-one percent increase), and sharing values with one's firm (results in an eighty percent increase). The positive correlation between career perceptions and likelihood of staying was stronger for female respondents than for male respondents.

Conclusion

Equity by Design's work has confirmed that there are pitfalls that we need to address to stave off attrition from the field and promote equitable demographic representation within architecture's ranks. However, this work has also established a roadmap for transcending the original goal of equitable representation by re-making the field with equity as our guidepost. To do so, firm leaders, our professional organizations, and practitioners must work together to ensure that the following ingredients for a satisfying career in architecture are available to all design professionals:

1. Equitable pay practices
2. Clear criteria for promotion and performance evaluation
3. Firm leaders who walk the talk by modeling work-life flexibility
4. Shared values between firms and individuals
5. Relevant, meaningful, and rewarding work
6. Access to firm leaders for mentorship, coaching, and feedback
7. Strong relationships within one's firm

Infographics by Atelier Cho Thompson. Courtesy of Equity by Design.

PARTNERSHIPS IN PRACTICE

AN INTERVIEW WITH BILLIE TSIEN

Billie Tsien, partner of Tod Williams Billie Tsien Architects (TWBTA), was the keynote speaker at the 2017 AIA Philadelphia Women in Architecture scholarship fundraiser, proceeds of which went to a graduating female student from the Charter High School for Architecture + Design in pursuit of the student's design degree. Following Billie's lecture, interviewers Franca Trubiano and Ramona Adlakha continued the conversation in discussing her design values, growth as an architect, and the importance of partnerships in practice.

Q When did you decide you wanted to study architecture and wanted to be an architect?

A Unlike many people who have been very clear about an interest in architecture, I think I've always been very unclear. I would say that I sidestepped into the study of architecture. I had actually wanted to be a graphic designer because I liked the idea of creating order.

I was in California and somebody said, 'Well UCLA is really cheap. They don't have a graphic design program but you could study architecture." So, it was completely a fluke. I went to the first architecture meeting where they bring in all the students and where they used to ask you to look to the left and look to the right, while saying that the person beside you probably wouldn't be there in another six months. But, instead of doing that, they handed out a piece of paper and with all these prospective students, they said, "Put the paper behind your backs and tear an elephant." So, we're all doing this, tearing an elephant out of paper.

The message was that with architecture you have a kind of idea but you're not completely in control of how it's actually made or produced. It's not about the singular control that you learn about when you're in art school, because I had studied art as an undergraduate. Rather, it is something that is both in your control and out of your control. And I found that very interesting. And so, I went to architecture school at UCLA where I also realized that I love studio culture. I loved the camaraderie; I loved being in the studio late at night with people. I sidestepped into architecture not really having it as a particular goal and finished architecture school. I still wasn't totally sure I wanted to be an architect.

It took me probably about five or six years of working, maybe even more, before I felt completely committed to architecture. The thing that I didn't like in practice was that things always seemed to be coming undone even as you felt like you were finishing them up. The great thing in school is that you work really hard on a project and it's done. But in practice, even as we're finishing up a project, there are things that previously seemed right, that now need adjusting. That was a hard thing to get used to, until I started to understand that the resultant of architecture is not only a sort of object or thing, it is also the process of making that thing happen. So, when I began to accept that the process was also equally important, then it was easier for me to accept the idea that when you're done, you're not really done.

Q You have worked with your husband Tod Williams since 1977 and have been in a professional partnership since 1986. How would you characterize this partnership? Do you each practice differently?

A In 1977, I came to New York and got a job with Tod, who had graduated from Princeton in 1965 and worked for Richard's office for about six to seven years, after which he started his own practice. Tod had been working at his own practice for about four years before I came into the office as a temporary employee to do renderings for a young architect's competition. There I was, in the peak of summer with no air conditioning and with colored pencils as my main tools. It was truly another time.

I had never worked in an architect's office before. I really came in knowing nothing but having this sort of freedom of not knowing a whole lot. At that time Tod had a partner and a couple of other people who were working for him. Over time we became personally involved, married in 1983, and became partners in 1986. I would

FIGURE 1. Tod Williams & Billie Tsien in their Central Park Studio, 2007.
© Michael Moran

FIGURE 2. Williams & Tsien, 2010, inspecting unfinished blocks of Ramon gray and gold limestone at a quarry in the Negev desert, Southern Israel for the Barnes Foundation façade. Photography courtesy of Tod Williams Billie Tsien Architects | Partners.

say the partnership worked because we are very different from each other. This allows us to work on every project in parallel where we don't step on each other's toes because we are not standing in exactly the same place. I think our values are agreed upon and we are looking for the same thing but we find very different ways of getting there. I think he generally will make a statement and I will edit it and shift it, so it's a dialogue, which moves back and forth.

Q You have been quoted as saying that you do not practice as a single practitioner but as a collaborator alongside your husband. What are some ways, which you feel, have made you an effective collaborator in the field?

A I think anyone who is in practice understands that you don't do anything by yourself. There has been, and continues to be—because we all like to think of romantic heroes or heroines—this idea of a sole Creator. But life is more complex and nuanced. Relationships that one has in the studio and to the work are very important, and we feel everybody is in some way shifting and changing the final result. I think the work that we do, if I were not involved, would be very different. I think Tod would say the same. He is, strangely enough, in certain ways interested in more ambiguous and complicated space, and I'm probably interested in something that is simpler. In terms of the way we collaborate, it is truly a conversation.

In terms of how we collaborate, we collaborate in a special way with the people who are actually building or providing us materials, we're constantly learning from them. We always go to a quarry because we learn so much about the material and the place where it's made. We go to brick factories because there is such an embedded and deep knowledge there, which can only make our work better. That's another form of collaboration. Of course, you're also collaborating with the client because you're trying to understand what they are saying and what they mean, which is often not the same thing.

Q The Obama Library project, which is currently underway by TWBTA, is the first with a woman as the lead architect, not to mention the first woman to co-design a United States presidential library. How has working on this project unfolded? Have there been many obstacles to overcome to bring to project to fruition?

A Well, yes. I think any project with a huge sense of ambition and an incredible legacy to express is both the project of a lifetime and incredibly difficult. One of the great things about the project is that it is not only about presenting a legacy. In fact, the actual archives are not going to be on site. They will be digitized, and the space will be used for classrooms and programming that will teach young people both from the United States and the rest of the world about civic engagement. It will give people the tools to change their world. That's a pretty big ambition, as you can imagine. So how do you do that? Everything that you do has to have both a use and a meaning. The obstacles are those things that inspire us. None of these things are easy. This is not the standard presidential library with a big archive and a museum off to the side. There is a museum—which will be a very important part of the experience—but there are a whole series of classrooms, a broadcast studio, and a productive garden. It's going to be something that hasn't been done before, so it's exciting. And certainly, it's exciting to be the first woman to co-design this. Yet, everything that the Obamas have done, in many ways, are firsts, so I am not surprised, but I am really honored.

Q Given the context of the post-Obama years, might there be some additional urgency, from an architectural perspective for the project to communicate issues of value?

A I think they see the project in the long view. It took how many hundreds of years for an African-American to become president? We see this as a 250-year-old building. And I personally feel that the values represented are terrifically important. I would say that in terms of the Obama Foundation, they are looking towards the future. What is being expressed are values that are ever more important now. But these are values that will also be important fifty years from now, and a hundred years from now. There's a sense of calm from the Obama Foundation, which is more than I might have because I personally wake up every morning feeling a little crazy. Theirs is a calmer idea of what the goal is, rather than it being a reaction.

Q TWBTA's projects embody exquisite craft with deference to material expression. In your practice, how do you begin to seek out materials in the design of a project? Are there particular materials that inspire you?

A It's like looking in your refrigerator and going to the farmer's market. Certain things you look at are in the refrigerator and maybe you have used them before. For instance, we are very interested in weight and solidity, so stone or masonry is somehow always there in the refrigerator. When you're making a meal, you pull out the stuff that you know because you know you can do something pretty good with it. But then you also go to the farmers market where you can become inspired by something that you hadn't expected. This helps you make something more amazing.

So, I would say that there are certain things that we rely on in an overall sense, and then we look at art, reflect on our travels, and break ourselves of the blinders and habits we have to bring another level of inspiration. I think the fabric of a place we are building in is always the first step in a recipe for what you're going to cook. By fabric, I mean the palette, the material, the sense of culture and place. I feel there are very different ways of creating a sense of place, but the specificity of making a building feel like it belongs is very much at the heart of everything that we do.

Q At the AIA Philadelphia Women in Architecture talk, you were quoted as saying, "One of the things we need to do as women in practice is understand what are the powerful elements that are within ourselves, which are not necessarily part of the mainstream." Can you expand on this?

A I think we have incredible strength. When I was younger, people always told me to speak up. And I found myself doing that to a young woman at Yale when I was there on a jury. I realized that we have important things to say and we don't need to scream them, but we need to be able to feel that we can say things without asking for permission. I think that's really important. I have noticed that as women, we all do this. We say, "Sorry, but …" and it's as if we are saying sorry to disturb you or sorry but I have an idea. I worked very hard not to say sorry all the time. I also work very hard to not be the loudest voice in the room, but to be able to make myself be heard. I think all women can do this. I think you can speak quietly and other people will back down but you have speak quietly with conviction. I also think that there is a kind of generalization that we're taught to

Q Given professional and educational environments and given that we're not likely to have a large degree of governmental support across the board anytime soon, can you share some insights about how more experienced or even young women can challenge the professional infrastructure to create more integrative structures and organizations that allow women to not have to make that choice?

A I think it begins at home. I don't think that the American Institute of Architects (AIA) is going to do it, and I don't know that architecture can do it. I would say it starts with an office and the commitment to making sure that there is paid parental leave. I think architecture firms need to commit to doing that at the very beginning. So, what I'm pretty much saying is that I think it needs to start locally. It's not something that comes from the top but something that comes from what's around you.

Q Are there any particular influences or inspirations that have shaped your career?

A Fiction. I read all the time. And I actually never read anything about architecture. I read novels because they are stories about people. I feel like stories about people tell me about architecture in an indirect way, which I think goes back to how I started architecture. I sidestepped into it, and I feel stories are a sidestep into making places for people.

Q You have had a prolific career both teaching and practicing architecture. At the same time, you have championed for the advancement of women by supporting scholarships, teaching, public engagements, as well as being a role model for young women everywhere. What advice would you give those who seek to enter the profession today?

be empathic. That sense of empathy is what gives humanity to our work and allows people to have a unique personal connection to it. I also feel that for me that's why the experience of what we do is my first concern. Much less so the sense of it as an object, I really care about the experience. I think those are things that are actually quite particular to many women. Finally, I think the ability to be aware of other people and others things and deal with many different things at same time is a particular strength that we have as women and should be valued.

Q What are some ways in which young women today can begin to prepare themselves for a career in architecture? Do you think schools are doing enough to prepare young women for the demands and politics of the workplace?

A Luckily, a career in architecture is very long. I'm not particularly sure what a school can do, but I think one of the things we can do as women who are teaching and practice is to teach, support, and mentor other women. I think one of the ways we can do this

when we participate in crest, but also in meetings in an office, is by making sure others are being heard. We need to support each other.

Q Do you think the profession is doing enough to address the issues of equity and gender balance?

A I think the profession has to because I don't think our government will ever do it. I think we have to provide a fair and equitable ability to take care of members—both male and female. We need to take care of family issues and child care in whatever way we can because that is the real reason why there is a problem with the gender balance. People progress with their careers, however, it's always a woman's choice when you have a child and a family, or whether you become a serious architect. That becomes a choice, but that shouldn't be a choice. There have been so many women who have had to make a choice to focus on architecture rather than a family, and that shouldn't have had to be the case.

A Jump in with your whole heart. It's like any big decision, it's like having a child, you just jump in. Sometimes you get down, but you just keep swimming. I think it's actually a great profession because you are serving people. Serving people is not about art, which you can sometimes achieve along the way, but it's an incredible way to work. This is a hard idea to accept, but if you can get satisfaction from solving somebody else's problem, then I think it's a great profession.

Q What can you offer us to help us vision a better narrative and a narrative that is empowering for the next five years for this profession, given everything that's happened in the recent past?

A Not just citing the #MeToo movement because I think it's much more than that, I think it is a very important moment in time because we realize that you don't have to smile and pretend like nothing happened. And it's certainly a very good thing for women entering practice! It's interesting now because it has been several generations where men have seen their mothers go to work, which

I think is a very good thing. It's not unusual for men working in their field right now to experience this, as it's likely their mothers had a job and maybe even their grandmothers. There's a certain amount of breaking down people's expectations and also breaking down woman's expectations for herself. It's not always a woman's job to make things nice, which gives us great freedom and power.

One of the things that President Obama talks about is standing on the shoulders of others and other people's stories. I think that young women are embracing feminism and are even unafraid to use the word. That's a very powerful tool to bring into the profession. It's a very interesting and exciting time, even though politically and environmentally it feels like a fraught time. I think women have the ability to do great good.

FIGURE 5. Lefrak Center at Lakeside, Prospect Park, 2013, Brooklyn, NY
© Michael Moran

FIGURE 6. The Annenberg Light Court, The Barnes Foundation, 2012, Philadelphia, PA
© Michael Moran

Building Futures is dedicated to showcasing the rapidly evolving character of women in architectural practice. As a professional discipline, the architect's remit is substantially dependent on the needs of clients and the knowledge of collaborators, consultants, commercial interests, and constructors. Moreover, as designers of the built environment, architects are directly impacted and constrained by the forces of global capital that subtend all aspects of a project's development. Negotiating, contracting, and building requires a skill of heroic proportions in what is still one of the most conservative of industries. The three articles in this section speak to the different ways that women have intuited their practice in this highly challenging environment. They address with whom, for whom, and to what end women choose to engage in the business of building. Blumberg reminds us of the ethical values that are imparted to the discipline when one adopts an expanded definition of 'client,' Dubbeldam communicates the power of innovation and self-mastery as a means of gaining independence over the limitation of traditional building, and Dosso promotes the continued empowerment of a community of women builders from the margins of architecture—that is, the construction site.

building futures

BUILDING
A NEW MODEL

Shirley Blumberg

Growing up in South Africa, I enjoyed a well-worn joke that was sadly true, "As an airplane approaches landing in Cape Town, the pilot announces local weather and time, and advises passengers to set their watches back eight hours and twenty years." This joke is an accurate reflection of the country where I was born and raised during the 1950s and '60s. South Africa was known as a country of stark contrasts. It was a highly conservative country of privilege and extreme injustice. The role of women in middle class, white society was staunchly traditional, and other than being a teacher, there were no professional role models. There certainly weren't any female architects.

I never met, and had never seen, any professors who were women during my architectural studies in Cape Town. I could count on the fingers of one hand the number of my fellow female students. After my third year, I moved from Africa to London, England, and a year later I emigrated to Canada where I completed my studies. The transition from South Africa to England to Canada was both exhilarating and intimidating. And yet, at

the University of Toronto, I could still count the number of women in my class on one hand.

As an architect and founding partner of KPMB Architects, I practice with my partners of thirty years—Bruce Kuwabara and Marianne McKenna. I'm grateful and consider myself fortunate to have taken this journey. I live and practice in Toronto, a city where fifty-three percent of the population is foreign born. It's one of the most heterogeneous and diverse cities in the world. Two of the three partners of KPMB are women. The firm's success is based in large part on a model that's non-hierarchical and collaborative. It's one we have invented, refined, and grown up with over our three decades together.

Jane Jacobs was living in Toronto when I arrived and her influence on our city was transformative. Today, it seems obvious that a functioning society is based on inclusivity and diversity, one where all voices are heard. Jacobs noted that, "Cities have the capability of providing something for everybody, only because and only when, they are created by everybody."[1]

As architecture is produced in the always unfinished and ever evolving fabric of the city, it's imperative that the voices of women architects participate in the collective conversation and expand the discourse about our built environment.

Contemporary challenges such as climate change, overpopulation and migration, social and economic inequity, diversity, and the scarcity of financial and natural resources have become increasingly acute. We live in a time of crisis and opportunity As our existing societal structures undergo stress and rupture, the criteria architects must address are well beyond cultural and artistic, they're wide ranging and very serious.

Architects must have the ability to synthesize and reconcile opposing issues. These skills have always enabled us to solve complex problems. KPMB addresses these challenges in a direct and collegial way, fully aware that the opportunity is to positively impact the lives of those who will inhabit our buildings. Put simply, we're committed to creating a better quality of life for people. As architect and visionary Buckminster Fuller noted, "You never change things by fighting the existing reality. To change something, build a new model that makes the existing model obsolete."[2]

An even more revolutionary model of practice is evolving internationally. The recent Pritzker Prize winners, Alejandro Aravena from Elemental in Chile (2016) and Rafael Aranda, Carme Pigem and Ramon Vilalta from RCR Architects in Spain (2017) provide clear evidence. At the 2016 Venice Biennale curated by Aravena—*Reporting from the Front*—the focus was on an alternative model of practice that truly grapples with the complex challenges we face collectively. Many of the national pavilions addressed issues of the global crisis in affordable housing.

I believe women architects have a major role to play in this. An article in the May 2017 issue of the *London Review of Books* entitled "Women in Power," voiced insights that I found to have great resonance and relevance to operating in our male dominated profession.

> You can't easily fit women into a structure that is already coded as male; you have to change the structure. That means thinking about power differently … thinking collaboratively about the power of followers not just of leaders … the ability to be effective, to make a difference in the world.[3]

Beard cites *Black Lives Matter* as an example, one of the most influential political movements of the last

FIGURE 1. Ponderosa Commons.
© Nic Lehoux.

few years, founded by Alicia Garza, Opal Tometi, and Patrisse Cullors, three women who, despite the enormous impact of their work, are hardly household names. *Idle No More* is an Indigenous Canadian movement founded by four women: Nina Wilson, Sheelah McLean, Sylvia McAdam, and Jessica Gordon. Its mandate focuses on Indigenous rights, stopping environmental degradation, and stands against economic and social inequality.

I believe architecture must be a powerful tool for positive change in society. In that sense, a 'model' becomes a 'movement.' It can impact issues of social justice, inequity, and limited resources.

Architects are problem solvers: we're trained to invent solutions for complex social, environmental, economic, technical, bureaucratic, and often contradictory issues. To imagine innovative design solutions, we must also engage in an effective and authentic process of community consultation and research. We must listen, fully understand, and define the problem that requires an architectural solution.

Below are four recent projects I have completed. All were achieved with unusually limited schedules and construction budgets—although this is coincidental and not mandatory. The tight budgets forced us to rethink our design approach. All four have had a profound and positive impact on the diverse communities they serve.

Project 1 - Ponderosa Commons
Close to 1,000 acres in size, the University of British Columbia (UBC) campus is located on the western tip of Point Grey Peninsula in Vancouver, surrounded on three sides by magnificent Pacific

north-west forests and the ocean on the fourth. Ponderosa Commons is the prototype and the first of five new mixed use residential academic hubs initiated by the University for its large commuter campus. The project integrates student housing, academic and social space, and retail services to produce a vibrant 24/7 precinct. UBC Student Housing and Hospitality Services (SHHS) builds and operates student residences on a for profit model, and accommodates more than 9,000 students at the Vancouver campus. SHHS, in collaboration with UBC Campus and Community Planning, UBC Properties Trust (project management and development), and several academic departments comprised the multi-stakeholder client group for the project.

Phase one comprises two buildings on adjacent sites south of University Boulevard on the west side of campus, Phase two is located opposite on the north side of the landscaped boulevard. Phase one East and West houses the Audain Art Centre and Geofluvial Lab programs respectively. These academic facilities are integrated with approximately 600 student residence beds, a learning Commons, study rooms, fitness facilities, a collegium for commuter students, and a cafe. Phase two comprises approximately 500 student beds and amenities including a small food market and a multi-purpose event space off a below grade landscaped courtyard. UBC's Education Department is the academic program and includes classrooms, seminar and study rooms, and faculty offices.

The greatest challenge of the 600,000sf LEED Gold project was to meet the unusually constrained budget and schedule. Phase one was constructed for \$208/sf, and Phase two for an even lower construction budget of \$183/sf. This challenge became the opportunity and driver for the project design. Our strategy was to work closely with the Construction Managers and their trades during the design and documentation phases, and to engage in a constant value engineering process. In effect, we reverted to a 'master builder' role in order to understand the most economical and innovative way to design our cladding systems of precast concrete and curtain wall. This approach extended to all building systems and finishes.

The white brick modernist buildings on campus became our visual reference for the range of white and charcoal insulated precast panel cladding system we developed. Not only was it extraordinarily cost effective (subsequent academic hub buildings use the same system) and quick to install, but its thermographic performance was a hundred

percent. For the student residence rooms, the smooth interior face of the sandwich panels were simply painted, saving the cost of drywall finishing. Rough-sawn western red-cedar used on grade-level soffits bring warmth to the material palette, while color and graphic composition were used as design strategies to animate the architecture and provide a collective sense of place. The curtain wall cladding of the Audain Art Centre integrates colors inspired by the mixed media works of Ian Wallace, a former professor of art at UBC, and an influential artist recognized for his role in influencing the renowned photo conceptual art practice of former students Jeff Wall and Stan Douglas.

Landscape played an important role in the precinct. University Boulevard is predominately recreational landscape, for pedestrians and cyclists. Each of the three buildings include outdoor courtyards to the south and north, and an extensive new system of pedestrian pathways integrates the new precinct into this area of campus, creating a well-developed and well used public realm. Ponderosa Commons has been highly successful, socially and academically, and has exceeded expectations as a business model for SHHS. Despite being the most expensive residence on campus, it is the number one choice for students. The budget constraints inspired a rigorous

FIGURE 2. 150 Dan Leckie Way.
© Tom Arban Photography Inc.

and collaborative design process that produced great value, and a learning and living environment that has resonated with both students and faculty.

Project 2 - 150 Dan Leckie Way

Our client, Toronto Community Housing (TCH), is the largest social housing provider in Canada, and the second largest in North America. They partnered with private developers, Context Development, to realize this project, which addresses a critical shortage of affordable rental family housing in downtown Toronto. Specifically, this project was planned and designed to provide social housing on land opened by TCH, in a rapidly developing precinct of disused former rail tracks south of downtown, Railway Lands West.

Our goal was to design a collective home for low income and diverse families that would foster a real sense of community, health and well-being, and dignity. It is the only affordable housing building in a neighborhood of market condominiums. Occupying an entire city block, the project comprises an eight-to-ten-story podium and a thirty-five-story tower. At the podium, stacked grade related units animate the street fronts, with a coffee shop on the corner facing the public park. All parking and servicing is accommodated within the podium, the roof of which serves as a generous landscaped outdoor amenity space for the residents.

Large three- and four-bedroom family units occupy the podium, and are designed within a unique skip stop building section, which minimizes the number of internal access corridors and allocates that additional 'found' space to the units. This approach produced unusual and diverse unit layouts with great access to natural light and views, a combination of two-story, and through units. It also produced a light-filled access corridor on each exterior podium façade, unique amongst the more traditional multiple housing typology of Toronto.

One- and two-bedroom units, better suited to the constraints of a small floor plate, are located in the tower. In all, this project delivers 430 units of subsidized social housing. Social amenities include a multipurpose event space that is used by residents and open to the local community, urban agriculture, communal kitchen, games room, lounges, and laundry facilities, some distributed in each wing of the podium and most located on the rooftop landscaped courtyard, animating what has become the shared outdoor living room for the residents.

In order to meet TCH's construction budget standards, conventional exterior cladding systems of precast concrete and window wall with a clear glazed and spandrel glass pattern were designed as a graphic composition. Color was strategically added to animate the public spaces and provide orientation and identity in a large building complex. This building has become a flagship and a model for TCH housing, and has become much more than an apartment complex. It has become a vibrant community.

Project 3 - Robert H. Lee Alumni Centre
The Alumni Society of the University of British Columbia (UBC) commissioned this ambitious project to develop a new home in a prominent central location on campus. The building functions as a welcome center for visitors, a home base for over 325,000 university alumni, and a place for current students, faculty, and administration and the local community to use. This is the place on campus where the entire university related community can come together. The building also embeds references to the deep history of this location in its design. All Vancouver, including the Point Grey university campus, is located on unceded traditional territory of the Musqueam First Nation. Specific design strategies acknowledge this.

The 40,000sf pavilion building is designed as a viewing platform from which, at every level, the visitor gains unique perspective views of the beautifully verdant campus environment, located in its distinct Pacific Northwest coastal context. In Vancouver's predominantly gray and rainy climate, the exterior white porcelain-fritted glazing changes dramatically in appearance when the sun shines—a soft translucent surface becomes bright white and reflective of the blue sky. Light and shadows of the frit pattern accentuate this effect on the interior. During the day, the pavilion is a pristine frit glass angular form. At night, the warmth of the local British Columbia wood used extensively on the interior reveals the generous atrium that links all three floors with a sculptural wood stair, the form of which references the two headed serpent—the origin story of the Musqueam people. The atrium is flooded with natural light, and as one ascends the stairs, a heritage elm tree anchors the east end of the building. The stairs are designed to visually link the heritage tree (one of the last surviving Dutch elm trees in this location) with the view to the west of the campus.

A multi-functional celebration hall affords almost 360-degree views to the surrounding campus on the second floor. The University Board of Governors third floor meeting room is located at the western end of the pavilion, with spectacular views of the

FIGURE 3. Robert H. Lee Alumni Centre. © Nic Lehoux.

campus—a constant reminder of the institution they govern. At grade, the building is highly transparent, porous, open, and welcoming. A popular cafe, fireplace lounge, study spaces, and library are well used by visitors, students, alumni, and faculty. Western red-cedar soffits shelter outdoor sidewalk cafe tables and chairs. The feature stair extends down into a below-grade level, bringing abundant natural light to the University's innovation hub, which serves current and future alumni.

The client, UBC Properties Trust (project managers and developers) established a highly constrained construction budget target of $310/sf for a small institutional building of this quality. Much like the process that we developed on Ponderosa Commons, we worked collaboratively during the design and documentation phases of the project with the Construction Manager and their trades to meet these financial constraints. The project has been very well received both within the university community and the larger city community, and has become an inclusive and active heart of campus social life.

Project 4 - Fort York Public Library

The Toronto Public Library system is the largest in North America and one of the most used per capita in the world. The new Fort York Branch has become an important community hub in a highly diverse and rapidly evolving new neighborhood in downtown Toronto. Our libraries truly function as urban living rooms and are used by many Toronto residents as their 'third place,' particularly as apartment dwelling is increasingly the norm downtown, for couples and young families.

The Toronto Public Library is arguably one of our most progressive urban institutions. In addition to traditional library functions, which include lending books, magazines, and videos, their programming is hugely successful. It includes children, adult, and community programs, author speaker series, three-dimensional printing, computers, and digital film studios. Branch libraries also function as the first stop for new immigrants, providing assistance with information and services. As Toronto's population is fifty-three percent foreign born, and approximately 120,000 people move to the greater metropolitan area every year, this is a vital community service.

This project responds to a unique heritage context. It is located on what was once the original forested shoreline of Lake Ontario at the mouth of Garrison Creek. The industrialization and landfill of the waterfront shifted the shoreline significantly south. Pre-settlement, this area was Indigenous peoples' hunting and fishing grounds. It was one of the locations where the War of 1812 was fought, and

FIGURE 4. Fort York Public Library.
© Riley Snelling.

historic Fort York is situated immediately west of the site.

The heritage fort is buried within the existing fabric of the city, and we saw the opportunity to open both pedestrian access and views to the historic precinct.

City urban design guidelines suggested incorporating the library into the base of the adjacent residential building, but instead we designed it as a standalone pavilion, allowing several pedestrian pathway connections to the future park to the north, which affords direct access under Bathurst Street Bridge to the grounds of Fort York. The angular trapezoidal geometry of the pavilion building directly references the geometry of the ramparts of the fort, and the extensive use of wood in the interior of the building recalls the historic wooden cribbing found buried on site during the archeological investigation. Wooden barrack buildings circa 1812 were known to have been located on the site.

The second floor of the library is a complete surprise in the extraordinary views afforded of the Fort York heritage site and the city, and towards the lake. The new neighborhood is dense and diverse: it includes a range of housing from affordable social to market-rate residential apartment buildings. The library has become an incredibly well-used inclusive community center for all.

Grade level is open and transparent, setback from the upper level, which is clad in custom designed vertical perforated metal louvres to afford views in and out, and to control heat gain. On the west façade, the perforations are designed to represent one of artist Charles Pachter's illustrations from the *Journals of Susanna Moodie*—a book of poetry by Margaret Atwood who interprets Moodie's voice from her diaries. Susanna Moodie was one of Canada's noted early writers, who arrived in the country in 1832. Selected lines from Atwood's poems complete the integrated art installation.

Endnotes

1   Jane Jacobs, *The Death and Life of Great American Cities* (New York: Random House, 1961), 238.
2   L. Steven Sieden, *A Fuller View: Buckminster Fuller's Vision of Hope and Abundance for all* (Divine Arts, 2012), 259.
3   Mary Beard, "Women in Power," *London Review of Books* 39, no. 6 (March 16, 2017): 9-14, https://www.lrb.co.uk/v39/n06/mary-beard/women-in-power.

BEYOND THE CORPORATE LADDER

Nicole Dosso

Status Quo

Discussions concerning the underrepresentation of women in the field of architecture are not new. Research, surveys, and analyses covering this topic have been gathered and documented over the last decade. Concern with work-life balance, lack of role models, pay disparity, and challenges in career advancement are some of the key findings reported by women.

In 2016, the National Architectural Accrediting Board (NAAB), responsible for developing a system of accreditation for professional architecture programs, released an annual report incorporating statistics on gender.[1] The breakdown of degrees awarded was reported as forty-three percent female compared to fifty-seven percent male. This statistic represents significant improvement in the number of women graduates since the time I was a student more than two decades ago, but still requires improvement.

Around the same time, the National Council of Architectural Registration Board (NCARB), responsible for the development of standards for licensure, issued their report "NCARB by the Numbers." Their findings indicate that only thirty-five percent of newly licensed architects are women. In comparison to gender statistics of degrees awarded in the field of architecture, this represents a significant reduction. However, the statistics become even more alarming as you further analyze the findings and realize that only fifteen percent of female licensed architects are in positions that involve supervising emerging professionals preparing for their license.[2] The rapid decline of women as their role shifts from mentee to mentor directly correlates to the steadily diminishing number of women in positions of senior leadership.

These analyses prove there is a lack of representation of women in the field of architecture; starting in academia, in entry-level positions in the workplace, becoming a licensed architect, and subsequently culminating in a lack of women in leadership roles.

Gender Imbalance Across Disciplines

In 2006, the New York Times published an article titled, "Why Do So Few Women Reach the Top of Big Law Firms?" It noted:

Although the nation's law schools for years have been graduating classes that are almost evenly split between men and women, and although firms are absorbing new associates in numbers that largely reflect that balance, something unusual happens to most women after they begin to climb into the upper tiers of law firms. They disappear.[3]

In 2016, McKinsey & Company published the report, "Women in the Workplace." As part of their analysis, they indicated that women represent approximately forty-eight percent of the workforce filling entry-level positions. However, this figure steadily decreases across industries as women proceed into positions of senior leadership in corporate America at large.[4] I question why it is that when women begin to climb the corporate ladder they suddenly disappear? Perhaps, even more importantly, I ask what is being done to change this phenomenon, eliminate roadblocks, and pave a path for success? In September 2014, *Fast Company* published an article titled, "The Tallest Tower In The U.S. Is Being Built By A Woman." The opening line read:

> Forget about the starchitects—Daniel Libeskind and David Childs—who dueled incessantly over 1 World Trade Center's formal qualities and its poetic language. The architect who finally got the damned thing built is someone you've probably never heard of ... In other words, North America's tallest tower—which could easily have been the world's tallest—is being built by a woman.[5]

The article continued:

> The day I met her at SOM's offices on Wall Street ... She was effortlessly chic—more Paris than New York—in a brightly patterned Diane von Furstenberg wrap dress, steeply pitched white patent leather heels, and a string of silvery pearls.[6]

I was stunned on the initial read of the article that in 2014 the fact that I was a woman and the detailed description of what I was wearing was somehow newsworthy.

If I were to author an article about myself, I would highlight that I was junior in my career, I was leading a team of forty architects and pioneering head-on the most visible and politically charged project in the nation at that time. What I was wearing was irrelevant. I am certain the comment was unintentional and I was grateful for the recognition, but in a time where women are still underrepresented in the profession, I found the description of my choice of dress wear distracting.

I began working at the World Trade Center site within weeks of the events of September 11. In 2006, 7WTC became the first office building to be rebuilt in lower Manhattan. On the eve of the opening, I was ten years into my career and had been involved in only three projects. During those years, there were many professional lessons learned, perhaps the most telling for my career; tall

FIGURE 1. Nicole Dosso's photograph featured in the *Fast Company* article "The Tallest Tower In The U.S. Is Being Built By A Woman." Photography by Celine Grouard.

FIGURE 2. 1 World Trade Center construction scene. Photography by Timothy Schenck.

buildings take a long time to design and a long time to construct. Milestones cannot solely be measured by projects completed, but are often measured by significant moments in the course of a project. In September 2012, *Esquire Magazine* ran an article titled, "The Truth About the World Trade Center," where Tishman Construction's field superintendent—and my colleague—Michael Pinelli was quoted as saying, "The job is a marathon."[7]

In 2011, I completed my first marathon. I assure you, the eighteen weeks of preparation were strenuous and despite all the training, nothing will prepare you for those last five miles. All I could think about, after reading the quote, was that pretty much sums it up. The job truly was a marathon. Along the journey, there were numerous obstacles and challenges but giving up was never an option.

Choosing a path in the field of technical architecture has an added complication. Women are not only outnumbered in the architectural profession but are also faced with dealing with the challenge of being outnumbered as women in construction.

In 2010, the United States Department of Labor reported that women in construction constitute only nine percent of the total construction industry.[8] In addition to safety and health hazards faced by all construction workers, there are safety and health issues specific to female construction workers such as ill-fitting personal protective equipment, unhygienic sanitary facilities, and limited training for material handling. Women in the construction industry are also prone to discrimination, hostility, and sexual harassment. Each of these issues represents barriers to women both entering and remaining in the field.[9]

In 1999, one of my earlier assignments at Skidmore, Owings & Merrill (SOM) was the modernization of the Two Broadway building located in lower Manhattan. The building stripped to its structure would undergo a complete overhaul of its mechanical, electrical, and plumbing (MEP) systems, vertical transportation, and enclosure. Throughout the demolition phase I was regularly sent to the field to evaluate existing conditions. Floor call buttons had been decommissioned and an operator was assigned to a single service car to shuttle workers to and from floors. On a particular day I requested to be dropped off at an upper floor in the building. As I exited, I specifically recall telling the operator, "I need twenty minutes, don't forget to come back and get me." Following completion of the task, I returned to the service elevator to wait. As time ticked by, I concluded he had forgotten about me. The floor was abandoned, fall protection lined the perimeter where the curtainwall had been removed and the wind was blowing debris everywhere. I could hear the elevator car traveling up and down in the shaft so I started banging on the elevator door to no avail. Eventually I gave up and began descending down the stairs. At some point I noticed the hardware on the doors had been removed, preventing reentry. Twenty floors later, I was finally able to reenter. Upon entering the floor, I immediately noticed a couple of men sitting around smoking cigarettes—my arrival startling them. How do you get the elevator around here I asked? One of them quietly got up from his perch, walked over to the hoistway, pulled a wrench out from his back pocket and started violently pounding on the door. When the door opened he looked at me, "Now that's how you do it." As I exited the building my heart was pounding. I momentarily wondered whether this is what I had studied so hard for; nevertheless I returned the next day and then some to finish the job.

Fighting for Equality
In 1965, in an effort to combat discrimination in federally-assisted construction projects, President Lyndon Johnson under the Executive branch of Government put into effect an Executive Order titled 11246.[10] The focus of this order:

> Prohibits federal contractors and federally–assisted construction contractors and subcontractors, who do over $10,000 in Government business in one year from discriminating in employment decisions on the basis of race, color, religion, sex, sexual orientation, gender identity, or national origin.[11]

Over a decade later the Office of Federal Contract Compliance Programs (OFCCP) was established to enforce equal employment opportunity as outlined by this Executive Order.[12] In the late 1970s, OFCCP set a nationwide participation goal at 6.9% which was based on the overall population of women working in the construction industry at that time. OFCCP requires contractors and those partaking in federal assisted projects to engage in outreach to broaden the pool of qualified candidates in the construction industry to include minorities and women. Participation goals are a good faith effort and compliance is measured by whether a good faith effort has been met. Failure to meet the set goals does not constitute a violation. In the absence of a penalty the goal is often not met and subsequently there has been no increase in the participation of women in the construction industry since its inception.[13]

A Vehicle for Change
New York City (NYC) has historically been known for its diversity. It is not surprising, therefore, that city leaders would eventually advocate for a workforce that represents the makeup of their city. In 1992, following an initial disparity study conducted in the City of New York, Mayor David Dinkins made a commitment requiring twenty percent of city procurement be awarded to minorities or women; the goal, to ensure city contracts reflect the ethnic, cultural, and gender diversity of the city. Through this commitment, Mayor Dinkins created NYC's first Minority and Women-owned Business Enterprise also known as M/WBE.[14]

To benefit from these opportunities, a company must first pursue M/WBE certification. For NYC, the minimal requirements are as follows: a company must be at least fifty-one percent owned, operated, and controlled by a woman or a member of a recognized minority group, including Asian-Pacific, Asian-Indian, Black, or Hispanic. It must have been in business for a minimum of one year and located in New York City or surrounding counties, or have a substantial business presence in the city.[15] Two decades following the institute of the M/WBE program, a subsequent disparity analysis was conducted. As a result, Mayor Michael Bloomberg enacted Local Law 1 of 2013. Primary goals of this new legislation were to: help strengthen the Minority and Women-owned Business Enterprise program through expansion of certification programs, create online directories for certified firms, and eliminate the cap that listed M/WBE participation goals as applying to contracts valued at a maximum of one million dollars.[16] Most recently, current NYC Mayor Bill de Blasio has committed to doubling the number of certified M/WBE's from 4,500 to 9,000 by 2019; by 2021, award at least thirty percent of the dollar amount of City contracts to M/WBE's; and by 2025, award more than sixteen billion dollars to M/WBE's.[17]

It is undeniable that progress has been slow. Women and minorities continue to struggle in obtaining M/WBE certification, meeting the arduous prequalification requirements to compete for such work and ultimately to grow their businesses. However, each of these initiatives represents potential opportunities and positive steps forward in paving a path to success for both women and minorities in design and construction.

We need to continue to challenge those in the public and private sector; to provide women and minorities adequate support and reinforcement to start and maintain small businesses, encourage the elimination of good faith efforts, and enforce both accountability and percentage increases.

A Shift in Workplace

In 2013, *Architect* magazine interviewed Denise Scott Brown. One of the questions asked was what had inspired her to write the essay "Room at the Top." Written in 1975 the essay was not published for over a decade. Her response, "I wrote it because I was very angry ... I am told things like ... 'Would the ladies please move out of the picture so we can have the architects?' I would say, 'I am an architect,' and they'd say, 'Would you move out of the picture, please?'"[18] While reading this article, I was reminded of a similar moment I experienced in 2005. While leading the technical aspects of the 7WTC project, I was asked at a high level project meeting whether I was the scribe. I restate, it was 2005. Stunned, I calmly responded, "No, I am an architect." The look of disapproval on his face could not go unnoticed. He was clearly annoyed I was sitting at the table. I did not move and the meeting carried on.

The Brooklyn Navy Yards are not just a cool collection of repurposed warehouse buildings. Something bigger is happening here. This former shipyard, decommissioned in 1966, is today a catalyst focused on collaboration. Their mission is to "fuel New York City's economic vitality by creating and preserving quality jobs, growing the city's modern industrial sector and its businesses, and connecting the local community with the economic opportunity and resources of the Yard."[19] The Brooklyn Navy Yards, which houses 400 businesses is an incubator that sparks growth and collaborative opportunities, creating an environment that is breeding the next generation of innovators and entrepreneurs sharing knowledge, resources, and responding to the ever-changing world we live in.

The nature of work, the types of spaces in which work happens, and the top-down hierarchical pyramid that has been the roots of corporate America is disappearing. Small businesses are vital to the economic growth of cities. In the field of architecture, small businesses can and do have an important voice. Therefore, I pose the following question:

As women in architecture, should we continue to focus on how to climb the old hierarchical corporate ladder, a structure originating from a male military service, that is inefficient, irrelevant, and out of tune? Or should we be empowering women in design and construction to use their voices and find their own platform?

In a chapter titled "Quantum Leaps," Nathaniel Owings book, *The Spaces in Between*, published in 1973, discusses two subjects: People and Architecture, with a focus on Natalie de Blois.

> The subject of one chart was 'People,' a roster showing the gathering together of partners and associates, their longevity and their advancement through the hierarchy of the firm … The second chart of 'Architecture' graphically illustrated only the rarest of the rare, the project these young partners thought best represented their concept of SOM. The 'People' chart, with seventy-five tree rings, included just one woman: Natalie de Blois.

Long, lean, quizzical, she seemed fit to handle all corners. Handsome, her dark, straight eyes invited no nonsense. Her mind and hands worked marvels in design—and only she and God would ever know just how many great solutions, with the imprimatur of one of the male heroes of SOM, owed much more to her than was attributed by either SOM or the client.[20]

Owing's description of Ms de Blois continues:

> As a woman is wont to do—especially a handsome one—she married; and the conflict of career and home came into play, but not before four children and a year abroad on a Fulbright Scholarship had run their successful course. Without ever missing a beat in the rhythm of her all-out contribution to SOM, she asked for a change of offices to Chicago, where her divorced husband was and the children could be shared. And there she still is, carrying the full load of one major design job after another, alone among all those men until later—much later.[21]

Top-down pyramids provide a singular path and are a shortcoming of hierarchical organizations. Formal hierarchy does not respond to a rapidly changing world and has proven to be gender biased across many disciplines. In contrast, a bottom-up approach provides individuals with multiple paths to grow, and empowers a more complex organizational system. Meshwork models are powerful, fluid, and complex. They grow organically and create an array of ways to connect. In the future, I predict large scale hierarchical business models will likely not become extinct; however, for such business models to remain relevant and compete with evolving

FIGURE 3. An architecture office scene, 1907. Courtesy of the New York Public Library.

technology, the next generation of entrepreneurs and clients who want to retain design firms that emulate their own think tanks and hierarchical business models will need to reimagine themselves to stay in the game. Today, we are at an important moment for the future of women in architecture.

Women-owned Business Enterprise supports entrepreneurship and is an important business development strategy for women in all fields. These unique opportunities, rooted in construction, have long been underutilized by architects and other disciplines. The post-war American corporate industrial hierarchy based on a military model has failed women.

Today there is a shift in how businesses are organized. Today's world is a world of meshworks. For women, Women-owned Business Enterprise offers opportunities that have not yet been fully explored and can be an instrument that can support entrepreneurship. Metrics should not solely be focusing on women's climb up the corporate ladder. Instead we should celebrate and encourage the percentages of businesses owned by women and their successes.

More than a decade ago, while attending a Real Estate Board of New York (REBNY) meeting, I had the following brief but impactful encounter. His face or name I do not recall; but what I vividly remember is his firm handshake and his pinstriped double-breasted suit. Upon meeting him I introduced myself as Nicole Dosso, an associate director at Skidmore, Owings & Merrill. He abruptly responded, "Excuse me?" I responded slightly louder. Again he abruptly responded, "Excuse me?" The third time I changed my tune. "My name is Nicole Dosso. I am a licensed architect in the State of New York." With that he shook my hand. "It is nice to meet you." It was an important lesson in the reality that hierarchical organizations focus too heavily on titles documenting the anticlimactic climb up the corporate ladder. Becoming a licensed professional architect, in the State of New York, was **my** accomplishment. Over and over, throughout the years, I witnessed senior leaders depart from their positions in large architectural and associated practices and were never replaced. Large hierarchical organizations breed robustness and duplication. To an untrained eye it might appear as if no disruption is taking place. However, comfort and status quo can leave leadership blind to recognizing modern day disruptions threatening their business.

A Blind Eye

For over 100 years the yellow taxicab was synonymous with New York City's urban landscape.[22] In 2011, a technological app called Uber was introduced to the city—disrupting NYC's century-old taxi business. Uber instantaneously transformed serviceability by focusing on convenience. Uber benefits the rider by eliminating unknowns and uncertainties. Uber also benefits the driver. Their mission to employees is clear, "Drive when you want, earn what you need."[23] Uber is a platform for an actor, actress, painter, or musician providing each the flexibility to substantiate their passions. It also provides opportunities for a parent coordinating around family commitments and is attractive to the entrepreneur, allowing an individual to be his or her own boss.

However, it is interesting that even progressive concepts struggle with gender and ethnic diversity. Based on data collected as of March 2018, Uber reported that women are underrepresented in their workforce. They acknowledge that achieving diversity and inclusivity requires transparency and a conscious effort to change the status quo. Uber recently announced on their website that they have created a new role of Chief Diversity and Inclusion Officer. Such roles that focus on championing and accountability are the key to success.[24]

The starchitect, a term given to famed architects, once represented the largest threat to hierarchical architectural organizations. Today it is the likes of Google, Amazon, WeWork, and Sidewalk Labs who are developing and influencing our cities. For architects, technology companies represent a modern-day disruptor that will present a significant impact to organizations that are not nimble.

WeWork, a company that mainly focuses on providing shared workspace whose mission is to build a community, "A place you join as an individual, 'me,' but where you become part of a greater 'we.'"[25] WeWork appeals to creators, leaders, self-starters, and entrepreneurs. WeWork is not only disrupting the real estate business but redefining the term 'workplace'—once the role of the architect.[26]

A Call to Action

The technological revolution has altered the organizational model of business and the way we work. In conclusion, today's world is a world of meshworks that favor entrepreneurs. By capitalizing on the shift in organizational business models, combined with an opportunity to utilize federal and state programs as a catalyst, women are empowered to become owners. Women-owned Business Enterprise represents an opportunity that has not yet been fully explored and can be an instrument that supports entrepreneurship. Metrics should not solely focus on women's ascension up the corporate ladder: together we should celebrate and encourage the percentages of businesses owned by women and their successes.

We should challenge each other to identify champions, embrace disruption, support collaboration, redefine the question, and reimagine our future. I am optimistic today, more than ever, that there is opportunity if we work together to find our stronger voices.

Endnotes

1   *NAAB 2016 Annual Report.* Washington, DC: The National Architectural Accrediting Board, 2016.

2   *NCARB By the Numbers.* National Council of Architectural Registration Board, 2017.

3   Timothy L. O'Brien, "Why Do So Few Women Reach the Top of Big Law Firms?" *New York Times,* March 19, 2006, https://www.nytimes.com/2006/03/19/business/yourmoney/why-do-so-few-women-reach-the-top-of-big-law-firms.html.

4   *Women in the Workplace 2016.* McKinsey & Company, 2016, https://www.mckinsey.com/business-functions/organization/our-insights/women-in-the-workplace-2016.

5   Karrie Jacobs, "The Tallest Tower in the US is Being Built by a Woman," *Fast Company,* September 29, 2014, https://www.fastcompany.com/3036116/the-tallest-tower-in-the-us-was-built-by-a-woman.

6   Ibid.

7   Scott Raab, "The Truth About the World Trade Center," *Esquire,* April 29, 2013, https://www.esquire.com/news-politics/news/a15344/world-trade-center-rebuilding-0912.

8   *Women in the Labor Force in 2010.* Washington, DC: U.S. Department of Labor, Bureau of Labor Statistics, January 2011, https://www.dol.gov/wb/factsheets/qf-laborforce-10.htm.

9   *Providing Safety and Health Protection for a Diverse Construction Workforce: Issues and Ideas.* National Institute for Occupational Safety and Health, 1999, https://www.cdc.gov/niosh/docs/99-140/.

10 Exec. Order No. 11246, 30 C.F.R. 12319 (1965)

11 Ibid.

12 "OFCCP By The Numbers," United States Department of Labor, accessed March 10, 2019, https://www.dol.gov/ofccp/BTN/index.html.

13 "FAQs on Nondiscrimination in the Construction Trades," United States Department of Labor, accessed March 10, 2019, https://www.dol.gov/ofccp/regs/compliance/faqs/NondiscriminationConstructionTrades_FAQs.htm; see also "Participation Goals for Minorities and Females," *Technical Assistance Guide for Federal Construction Contractors,* Office of Federal Contract Compliance Programs, https://www.dol.gov/ofccp/taguides/TAC_FedContractors_JRF_QA_508c.pdf.

14 Calvin Sims, "Dinkins Plan Gives Minority Concerns More In Contracts," *The New York Times,* February 11,1992, https://www.nytimes.com/1992/02/11/nyregion/dinkins-plan-gives-minority-concerns-more-in-contracts.html; see also *Making the Grade 2017.* Office of the New York City Comptroller, November 16, 2017, https://comptroller.nyc.gov/reports/making-the-grade/reports/making-the-grade-2017/.

15 "Minority and Women-owned Business Enterprise (M/WBE) Certification Program," City of New York, accessed March 10, 2019, https://www1.nyc.gov/nycbusiness/description/minority-and-womenowned-business-enterprise-certification-program-mwbe.

16 *Making the Grade 2017.* Office of the New York City Comptroller, November 16, 2017, https://comptroller.nyc.gov/reports/making-the-grade/reports/making-the-grade-2017/; see also "Local Law 129 of 2005," The New York City Department of Small Business Services Division of Economic and Financial Opportunity, 2005, https://www1.nyc.gov/assets/sbs/downloads/pdf/businesses/LL1.Flyer.6-13-17.pdf.

17 "Mayor de Blasio Announces Bold New Vision for the City's M/WBE Program," City of New York, September 28, 2016, accessed on March 10, 2019, https://www1.nyc.gov/office-of-the-mayor/news/775-16/mayor-de-blasio-bold-new-vision-the-city-s-m-wbe-program#/0.

18 Carolina A. Miranda, "Architect Interview with Denise Scott Brown," *Architect,* April 5, 2013, http://www.architectmagazine.com/design/architect-interview-with-denise-scott-brown_o; see also Denise Scott Brown, "Room at the Top? Sexism and the Star System in Architecture," in *Architecture: A Place for Women,* ed. Ellen Perry Berkeley and Matilda McQuaid (Washington, DC: Smithsonian Institution Press, 1989), 237–46.

19 "Our Mission," Brooklyn Navy Yard, accessed March 10, 2019, https://brooklynnavyyard.org/about/mission.

20 Nathaniel Alexander Owings, "Quantum Leaps" in *The Spaces In Between An Architect's Journey* (Boston: Houghton Mifflin, 1973), 263.

21 Ibid., 264.

22 Cecilia Saixue Watt, "'There's no future for taxis': New York yellow cab drivers drowning in debt," *The Guardian,* October 20, 2017, https://www.theguardian.com/us-news/2017/oct/20/new-york-yellow-cab-taxi-medallion-value-cost.

23 "Why drive with us," Uber Technologies Inc., 2019, accessed on March 10, 2019, https://www.uber.com/us/en/drive/.

24 Polina Marinova and Grace Donnelly, "Inside Uber's Second Annual Diversity Report," *Fortune,* April 24, 2018, http://fortune.com/2018/04/24/uber-diversity-report-2/; see also "Diversity and Inclusion," Uber Technologies Inc., 2019, accessed March 10, 2019, https://www.uber.com/about/diversity/.

25 "Our Mission," We Work Companies Inc., accessed March 10, 2019, https://www.wework.com/mission.

26 Murrye Bernard, "The Interloper: WeWork Upends the Conventional Architecture Firm," *Architect,* January 11, 2018, http://www.architectmagazine.com/practice/the-interloper-wework-upends-the-conventional-architecture-firm_o.

THE FUTURE IS ALWAYS NOW

Winka Dubbeldam

The dethronement of learning is one of the most exciting frontiers we are now crossing. In a virtual cyclotron, learning is being smashed into its primitives. Scientists are cataloging the elemental components for adaptation, induction, intelligence, evolution, and co-evolution into a periodic table of life. The particles for learning lie everywhere in all inert media, waiting to be assembled (and often self-assembled) into something that surges and quivers.[1]

The FUTURES panel of the "[RE]Form: The Framework, Fallout, and Future of Women in Design" symposium, held at PennDesign, University of Pennsylvania in spring 2017, has allowed me to reflect on my "life" path. Focused on identifying the critical role of women in architectural practice, the symposium investigated the role of academia, activism, and the future of women in design. It introduced the question of how to instigate a better, more equal, future. Being asked to consider how as women and architects we have been able to leverage our expertise to change what some consider to be one of the most recalcitrant of fields (architecture and buildings), was critical. The idea of 'change' was itself questioned; after all, feminism is not new; having roughly started in the late eighteenth century and being more than a century old. How is it then, that there is still so much to fight for? Possibly because architecture has traditionally been a predominantly male field, and while women have moved in and out of the field, they view the profession differently, both socially and culturally. And how might we deal with this in the future?

The 'future is always now' has been my motto for a long time: a statement that urges us to act, to be pro-active, and not to postpone. The attitude "Why not?" is best adopted when contemplating change, innovation, or leadership. It erases self-imposed and external limitations, doubt, and unnecessary rules. I started my "Why not?" phase as a student in Holland. Frustrated with the level of teaching, I escaped into new technologies and worked in real practice, where I met with Rem Koolhaas. Inspired by the rigor and forward thinking I found there, I changed my attitude and design work. Shortly after, having been one of the first in Holland to graduate in architecture with computer renderings and a small wire animation (1990), I moved to the United States in order to study the relationship between theory and digital design in architecture. Involved in many discussions and exposed to many points of view, my post–graduate year at Columbia University was crucial for my development as an architect. It was there that I was able to forge a way forward. I met Peter Eisenman at my thesis presentation, and after three years of working for him, I started my own office (1994), while also teaching in architecture programs at Columbia and Penn.

My early interest in three-dimensional digital design originated in my studies in art and sculpture, which taught me to think three-dimensionally rather than two-dimensionally. Rigorous art teachers pushed students to excel through hard work, starting over and over again, accepting nothing that was mediocre. It was sink or swim. From the fifteen students who started in first year, only five eventually graduated. It taught me to fight for excellence through rigor. When studying architecture, I could not think in flat surfaces and hence did not design using two-dimensional plans. Rather, I imagined three-dimensional shapes in my mind and, later, when designing with computers.

Soon after my arrival at Penn, I initiated 'Room 410'—a third year advanced Digital Design Studio that used Maya software, years before Columbia went paperless.

Women typically don't talk too much about what they do: they work hard and excel in what they do. By not engaging in a dialogue, however, they run the risk of being forgotten while others get the credit. Learning from that, women should be stronger advocates for themselves, their work, and definitely for each other. By taking the credit deserved, one is allowed to move forward. And as we know, it is only through dialogue that we learn.

Being a free spirit, I loved change and did not tie myself to one school of architecture. For eight years I taught one semester at Columbia and one semester at Penn, after which I started teaching at Harvard University. I quickly realized that having a practice requires discipline; I never taught at two places at the same time and never during the summer. This allowed me to catch up with work. While at Harvard, the then chair at Penn offered me a Practice Professorship, and asked me to initiate a new Second Masters program with him—a one-year post-graduate program called the Post-Professional in Design Program (PPD), with myself as director.

FIGURE 1. V33 condominium, NYC, seven stacked "villas."

After ten years of growing the PPD program, raising funds, and publishing student work, I was asked to apply for the chair position in the Department of Architecture at Penn Design. As chair, a whole new intellectual challenge opened up. After an initial orientation phase, I realized that it was important for Penn to claim a position and to state what role architects have, or should have, in the early twenty-first century. I initiated a symposium called, "The New Normal," organized in collaboration with my PPD colleagues Ferda Kolatan, and Roland Snooks. It proposed that after twenty years of digital design in architecture, a new platform was now established in which new forms of practice had emerged, and in which generative digital design had fundamentally altered the way in which we conceptualize, design, and fabricate architecture.

Indeed, virtually every aspect of our profession has been radically transformed. Innovations have not been restricted to questions of technology alone, they have also fueled a lively debate among leading educators, theoreticians, and practitioners in their respective efforts to understand the larger cultural ramifications triggered by this phenomenon. We asked participants to speculate on a new future—a "New Normal" platform—by looking at three topics; new assemblages, new niche, and the an-organic. Panels and their moderators, speculated on a future radical and innovative form of architectural practice—one that hybridizes, adapts, and transforms over the next two decades.

Ideal, one might say. So why, therefore, is architectural practice still so resistant to this platform of "The New Normal"? Is it because dialogue within architecture has reached a point of stasis, a plateau? It is clear that its 'problem-solving' attitude, usually based on cause and effect relationships, relies mostly on linear logic; a linearity that excludes the possibility of future provocations, of non-linear systems that allow for the emergence of new relationships, of a study of behaviors, and of system-based thinking. Architects, and the construction industry in general, tend to use the computer less to study complex systems, than to focus on organizational and representational implications and outcomes. This singular approach to using the computer restricts the intelligence of the structures created. As Kevin Kelly says:

> Co-evolutionary relationships from parasites to allies, are in their essence informational, ... dense communication is creating artificial worlds ripe for emergent co-evolution, spontaneous self-organization, and win-win cooperation.[2]

This is the challenge architecture faces; to move away from the purely organizational systematic approach into an intelligent registration of effects on form and smart formations. This pro-active approach means taking charge in innovation rather than following the norm—asking new questions rather than simply solving existing ones.

This also means that the architect no longer relies on the contractor to develop the innovative part of the building, but collaborates directly with manufacturers to innovate from the bottom up—becoming a partner in the research and development process. This fundamentally changes the work relationship between architect and contractor and puts the architect firmly back in charge. As a woman, I feel this attitude has helped me jump over some of the hurdles that otherwise would have been harder to overcome. It has also helped me to innovate in the design and fabrication of significant parts of our built work at our design studio—Archi-Tectonics—located in Manhattan.

To conclude, our focus at Archi-Tectonics is not on a recognizable 'signature', but to create a smart, optimized structure that emerges from comprehensive research and poetic rigorous precision. We value performance over form, design intelligence and efficiencies over style. We consider each project as an opportunity to develop innovative, original designs with a unique character and identity. While intuition and skill remain at the core of our design process, we supplant and supplement this knowledge with advanced digital form-generating and prototyping tools, merging into what we consider 'Digital Craft.' This methodology allows us to expand beyond accepted architectural conventions, opening the possibility of genuine innovation and discovery, while benefiting from the extensive construction knowledge we have developed over the years. Our work occupies a space between machine-like intelligence and organic embodiment—we like to think that our designs have 'character.' An identity that helps brand our client's new and existing companies, as well as create value. The following are some of our projects that demonstrate these ideas in [built] detail:

497 GW Loft Building, NYC - Twenty-Five Residential Lofts and Gallery/Retail Spaces (80,000 sq.ft.)

Concept-Crease-Code

The 497 GW Project, located on the edge of Soho, has a new eleven-story structure folding over a renovated six-story warehouse. The New York City Building Code is here re-interpreted; the horizontal plane of the traditional urban fabric is questioned by the insertion of a diagonal surface that bifurcates the façade plane. It integrates the strict building code setback into the new folded vertical landscape of the glass (west) façade. The crease as mediation and the glass inflections as spatial device allow for slippage between interior urbanism and urban privacy. The crystalline facets of the façade allow for it to move away from a separative two-dimensional membrane into a three-dimensional glass zone to be occupied and inhabited. Herbert Muschamp, famed architecture critic wrote in the *New York Times* "Dubbeldam's folds are philosophically as well as visually grounded ... [She] crystallizes urban complexity within the discrete architectural object."[3]

Smart Loft Building – Performance

The new building's innovative, angled-glass façade has been custom-designed. A performance analysis resulted in the differentiation between the façade's structural (steel) components and its waterproofing (aluminum) components (industrially designed and intelligent). This maximized the façade's

FIGURE 2. Ports 1961 Headquarters and Store, Shanghai, China.

FIGURE 3. 1:1 Prototype meditation space. Inscape, NYC.

performance and minimized costs and effort. Further analysis of the façade's structure led to the bending of glass panels in order to minimize forces and create completely transparent seams. The three-dimensional, folded-glass façade was a first in parametric design, in which electronic communication of three-dimensional computer drawings facilitated production between manufacturers in Barcelona, Hong-Kong, and Brooklyn, enabling them to fabricate the parts straight from three-dimensional files. This eliminated mistakes, resulted in a perfect fit, and optimized a fast manufacturing and installation process. The west glass façade and the heavy concrete floors allowed for passive solar gain, the addition of concrete cavity walls added mass, and reclaimed wood and aluminum insulated windows helped make this building sustainable and energy efficient.

Urban Lifestyle

The building's twenty-five lofts are designed as open loft plans with integrated amenities recessed in ceilings and walls; each loft is wired for music, Internet, satellite TV, and has a variety of heating and cooling systems. The large, modern, open-plan lofts offer an abundance of exterior spaces, balconies, and roof terraces, which are situated on both west and east façades. Residents can thus enjoy sunsets over the Hudson River from the comfort of their living space. Common amenities in the building include a shared guest apartment, gym, spa and pool, a screening room, and a wine cellar—offering a luxurious urban life-style in lower Manhattan.

V33 - Seven-Unit Condominium in Tribeca (45,000 sq.ft.)

Tribeca's landmark district, originally a warehouse area, received a new 'infill.' The choice to focus on the *quality* of Tribeca's traditional buildings, rather than *copy* them, was greatly appreciated by the NYC Landmark Committee. Extreme ceiling heights, tri-partite façade sub-divisions, durable natural materials, and façade alignments were some of the qualities and contextual issues examined. Since the design of façades on neighboring buildings vary greatly, the decision was made to extrapolate these differences onto a pixelated façade pattern, which negotiates the two neighboring façade rhythms. This now contextual texture of the V33 street façade was developed into a random 3D pattern of translucent stone and glass. The shift in material will allow the façade to constantly change over the course of a day; the translucent stone will glow by day in the interior, while by night it is reversed—thus transforming the façade over the course of a day and night.

Optimization

Here the traditional building has been de-laminated and optimized; the north street façade is considered a rather flat and textured stone and glass pixelation, while the south garden façade is deeply spatial, with large cantilevering sunrooms and terraces that create connected shaded interiors and generous outdoor areas. In the middle of the building where these two systems meet, we created spatial differentiation through floor folds and level changes—allowing for a separation of use without unnecessary enclosed spaces. Towards the street, spaces compress with lower ceiling heights; towards the garden, rooms open up with high ceilings and double height mezzanines. The garden south façade achieves continuity through a varying pattern of balconies, double height spaces, and shaded southern exposure.

Urban Villa

We considered the V33 building to not be a traditional apartment building, but rather a set of stacked *urban villas*. These villas are custom-designed with their own room lay-out, different exterior spaces, and double height areas. They vary greatly throughout the building. Because of their extremely generous size (between 3,500 and 5,000 sq.ft.), large outdoor spaces (terraces & gardens), and sometimes multiple floors, they create ideal urban living.

FIGURE 4. V33, NYC, seven stacked "villas," twelve-inch-deep terraces on South façade. Photography by Floto & Warner.

PORTS1961 Flagship Store - The Bund, Shanghai, China

Two important factors inspired the concept of the Ports1961 Shanghai Flagship Store, namely its history as an international port (boat building) and its famous Art Deco style. The store was also the first proto-space for future haute couture stores built worldwide for Ports1961.

Vessel

Inspired by the fluidity of old vessels, we introduced a silvery, recycled 'wood liner' within the space that holds the Ports' collection. The liner was CNC-milled from recycled wood obtained from a demolished old Chinese house. The wood was then rubbed with silver powder and oil, and no further finish was added. We combined the flowing silvery-gray wood that lines the edges of the space with pearly finished volumes in the middle of the space for exhibiting highlights of the collection in a gallery-like manner. Like an oyster, the rough outer walls appear first, but then reveal soft glowing silvery volumes, with suspended mannequin bodies, and custom designed bronze displays, lit from above and below. The lower platforms are CNC-milled smooth wood forms that have integrated lighting, felt benches, and hold the display units. Custom woven silk carpets follow the shape of the space—accentuating and creating comfort in an easy manner.

Display-Privacy

A golden metallic padded fabric-wall leads one into the private dressing rooms, where one finds ultra-comfortable large fitting rooms. The wood-lined fitting rooms have at the end, a full-height large mirror whose frame, 'frames' the client in an ingenuous set of pivoting mirrors, generously revealing all angles, and creating a multi-faceted crystalline space. The spaces are strategically and softly lit, without the harshness of a typical fitting room, making guests feel comfortable and look their best. For the proto design of future stores worldwide, a series of elements were designed. Archi-Tectonics developed suspended mannequins as 'sculpted' bodies, designed chrome-nickel bronze display tables lit by recessed light, integrated and padded felt benches in the low CNC-milled wood platforms, and added the TV-mirrors showcasing the latest fashion shows in Paris, Milan, and New York. Indirect LED lighting was used to enhance the space's fluid geometry, with lighting coves concealed in the floor and ceiling surfaces—thus, creating a contrasting glow on the clothing, accessories, and adjacent surfaces. The final effect is a rich, integrated environment that delivers maximum dramatic impact to a fluidly connected space.

FIGURE 5. Blaak Tower Rotterdam, 2019.

BLAAK TOWER - Residential Condominium and Retail

Stibnite Formations - The Tower as City

For this tower we looked at the self-referential shapes of stibnite formations: sulfide minerals that form spontaneously and result in unique forms, despite originating from identical systems. The tower's fragmented and slanted surfaces are designed to follow a spontaneous organizational system that follows a clear logic, while allowing for 'anomalies'. These anomalies are urban spaces pulled up from the city, which create semipublic lobbies on higher levels, such as gym areas, sky lobbies, meeting spaces, and a restaurant. As a result, the tower has a unique form with its own identity.

LEED Silver

The tower incorporates structural and material innovations and energy efficient systems. Specifically, the tower's silver frit pattern creates a 'climate veil' on the tower's façade, thus reducing heat gain on the warm elevations while cooling the overheated areas, and still creating un-obstructed views. Inside the building, the frit pattern is invisible; and glare and overheating are reduced. The tower design aims to achieve LEED Silver and an estimated rating of at least seventy-five. The towers react to the predominant west wind direction with natural ventilation, and the multi-story, glass sky-lobbies cool and filter the air, as 'green lungs' for the building.

Tapered Façades Fold to the Street

The tower's structurally glazed surfaces fold down and extend their surfaces wide to create generous spaces for easily accessible retail areas with above-grade parking. The tapered glass surfaces integrate city life into the tower, without the usual separation and control. Extended façades create an inviting street front with generous, comfortable public retail and hospitality spaces, while still creating a private entrance for the residences. Glass seams connect street lobbies to the upper sky-lobbies, which are lit, and especially at night express the shape and anomalies of the tower—serving as an icon for Rotterdam.

The photography featured in this article is courtesy of Archi-Tectonics unless otherwise indicated.

Endnotes

1   Kevin Kelly, *Out of Control, The new Biology of Machines, Social Systems and the Economic World,* (New York: Perseus, 1994), 85.
2   Ibid.
3   Herbert Muschamp, "ART/ARCHITECTURE; A Pair of Crystal Gems Right for Their Setting," *The New York Times,* January14, 2001. https://www.nytimes.com/2001/01/14/arts/art-architecture-a-pair-of-crystal-gems-right-for-their-setting.html. See also, Winka Dubbeldam, "GW497," Architect Magazine, March 18,2013, https://www.architectmagazine.com/project-gallery/gw497.

FIGURE 6. "Dome" meditation space. Inscape, NYC. Photography by Christian Harder.

PRACTICE MAKES PROGRESS

CONVERSATION BETWEEN JEANNE GANG + MARGARET CAVENAGH

Margaret Cavenagh, principal of Interior Architecture at Studio Gang, was a speaker at Penn Design's 2017 Women in Architecture symposium, "[RE]form: The Framework, Fallout, and Future of Women in Design." Following the event, Margaret and Jeanne Gang—Studio Gang's founding Principal—continued the conversation in a discussion, which evaluated the symposium's resonant themes with Studio Gang's organization, design process, and projects.

MC At Studio Gang, we think of ourselves as a collective of practitioners with different talents and perspectives, capable of discovering and creating more together than we could individually. We evolve and change as we need to. We play to our interests and strengths. This kind of diversity of experience and thought is really important, especially in architecture, which can be very homogeneous.

JG In architecture and elsewhere, we often see that a group of people with the same background and upbringing have a smaller chance of coming up with an innovative solution. A number of studies have demonstrated this, and I've found it to be true as well—the most interesting ideas come from a diverse group of people with different experiences all thinking about the same issue. Here in the Studio, we're deliberately cultivating that approach toward solving problems and identifying new ways of looking at the world.

MC It really does make the work much richer, and it's been exciting to see our teams, and the ideas they bring, develop. Their responses are varied, but they're all raising thought-provoking questions. Seeing them flourish shows the importance of giving everyone the support they need, of fostering the internal diversity that makes projects better.

JG Ideally you also foster a stronger debate. I think that one issue we face in architecture is that because we share strong cultural ties, we tend to agree with one another even though we may come from different backgrounds. So, it's especially important to make an environment in which it's comfortable for healthy debates to surface. Just bringing together a diverse group of people is not enough. There will still be barriers to drawing out those differences. You have to create an environment where it's okay to say what you think.

MC And to disagree.

JG Exactly—that's key. It's about encouraging a diversity of thought with a pluralistic approach. We work hard to create an office culture where everyone, even if it's their first day, feels comfortable sharing an idea. It doesn't matter where you are in the Studio structure, how long you've been here, or what position you might have. What we want to do is elevate the strongest idea, which can come from anyone. I've seen it happen, for example, when the newest person on the team has a really strong thought that's then built upon by everyone else. As the idea is adopted, pursued, and developed together, it comes to belong to the group. In this

way, the authorship of the project is shared because we've all contributed at different times to advance it further. Making it clear that we're equally called upon to participate and progress the work might entail a more thorough critique of an idea proposed by someone who has been with the Studio for a long time, like me. It also involves actively recognizing when someone has a brilliant idea. To create the best work you have to make it open to anyone to advance the idea, advance the project.

MC And we've always said, use whatever means are best to convey your idea. We have graphic standards, but we don't impose a rigid way of drawing or sketching. Instead, we encourage everyone to communicate in simple, straightforward ways that continue the conversation and progress it—like a simple paper model or a pencil sketch. We don't want to be constrained by always using digital tools or by "the way the Studio does something." We want to be free to convey the idea and move it forward, move it further.

JG That brings up a good point, because you always want to pick up the best tool in the toolbox. That could mean sophisticated, digital tools—it could also mean bond paper or colored pencil. Or it could mean conducting

FIGURE 1. Jeanne Gang and Margaret Cavenagh in dialogue with a client during a design meeting. Photography courtesy of Studio Gang.

FIGURE 2. Rowing teams from across the city make use of the WMS Boathouse at Clark Park (2013), located on the Chicago River's North Branch. Photography by Steve Hall © Hedrich Blessing.

interviews with people who will use the project—engaging individuals and communities. We all have different proficiencies, so our way of working is not always, technically, democratic, because if someone is especially skilled with a tool they should use it. Rather, it's about creating a democratic environment where the idea and the project are central, where the traditional hierarchies of architectural practice dissolve away and don't impede the progress of the work.

MC And we're actively breaking down those hierarchies.

JG We've taken a hard look at how we organize ourselves, both as an organization and a physical space. As an organization, we've turned the traditional pyramid structure upside down and created a more organic model that is based on a tree. The roots are our values and interests as a studio. Their strength and nourishment support the trunk and the branches of our leadership team, which in turn support the leaves and buds of our design teams and newest members, who are equally necessary to bringing life to the studio tree. It's a model that's meant to reorganize how people think about their responsibilities. We support

each other and each of us contributes to the system as a whole, always keeping the project at the center.

MC To do this, we're also very intentional about how we organize our physical space. We cluster our teams, with each team loosely located around a project table. This gives them a democratic, central territory where exchanges can be frequent and casual, rather than always needing to book a conference room or gather at the project leader's desk. There's an immediacy and horizontality that can be accomplished with this kind of workspace. It very much suits our process.

JG Thinking about diversity and outdated hierarchies, we should also say that we're looking outside our own office to consider how we can help the field as a whole to move forward. For example, academic schools that teach architecture can lack diversity, whether in terms of thought, background, or upbringing. So in addition to the usual practice of taking on student interns from these schools, we've also started to build alternative pipelines. We actively seek out interns from the high school system or just out of high school, as well as non-architecture majors, and give them exposure to architectural practice. Our goal is to build their understanding of what architects do and what they can do, and to foster a desire to learn more. Hopefully this encourages them to seek out architecture in their studies, to pursue it as a career path, and maybe one day to come back and work with us.

MC Yes, from a hiring perspective, it's so important to help expand the field in this way, because it means expanding the pool of talented designers. At Studio Gang, when it comes to hiring, we're always looking for excellence. This has turned out to mean that the office has always had nearly equal numbers of women and men. Today we're roughly 100 people and our teams have a slight predominance of women—which is unusual for architecture.

JG It's interesting, because as you say, our hiring choices are gender blind—they're based solely on the quality of an applicant's work and how they interview. Perhaps it's because our team already has a good gender mix that we're more attractive to women applicants. Also, our benefits are designed to support mothers, fathers, and different kinds of families, and to take into account that we're all likely to experience special circumstances at some point in our working lives. Margaret, you've been instrumental in that effort to support the full life of each person at the Studio with our benefits system. We're measuring ourselves against the field at large in order to attract top talent but also to leverage our influence industry-wide—to try to encourage the profession to change for the better.

MC Our office is now at a size where we can put pressure on the industry to practice better. I believe we're now in the top five percent of firms in terms of scale. We really do have the opportunity to influence the field.

JG One critical change we made this year was addressing the issue of gender pay equity. When the United Kingdom published a new report on gender pay gaps and their assessment tools—a set of calculations that any organization can use to comprehensively analyze their potential pay gap—we wanted to do the math and see if our salaries aligned with our commitment to equality. We used the tools and discovered that even though our numbers were significantly better than the UK architecture firms reporting, a small pay gap still existed between the women and men in our office. We fixed that with this year's raises and now have no wage gap as an organization! Achieving pay equity is foundational to raising respect for women and other minorities in the

workplace, and it's key to creating that kind of creative environment in which diverse talent develops new solutions. So it's absolutely essential that all of us in architecture eliminate these pay gaps. If we all do, as an industry we can lead the way in this transition. It's connected to other efforts as well, like expanding benefits for family leave.

MC At Studio Gang we currently offer four weeks of paid maternity leave, as well as additional paid leave categorized as short-term disability (even though pregnancy and new motherhood shouldn't be thought of as a disability!), and the opportunity to begin your leave period when you need to, not just when you have to. We also offer four weeks paid paternity leave, and as you mentioned, these benefits are open to anyone who is supporting a family, not just the traditional role of a mother or father—so it's moving the needle by supporting different family types. We talk about "actionable idealism" in our work—taking small, measured steps that add up to a greater positive impact. I think of our pay equity, benefits, and culture as an opportunity to practice actionable idealism at home, here in the Studio.

We're supportive of a work mode that is individual to everyone in the office. It's that kind of support that draws the best talent and allows that talent to produce the best project.

JG We work hard to create an environment that supports personal growth and creativity, and that's fun. The whole design of our office is based on being able to use architecture as a medium to pursue the things we love. We support each other's ideas and interests, and we participate in each other's lives and in the community. One especially fun example is our annual summer retreat at a camp in Wisconsin. We invite guests from different fields to share their work and perspectives through classes, and we share our own talents in informal workshops—from street art to weaving and watercolor and other forms of making. We offer a yoga class at the studio each week. We participate in Habitat for Humanity's Women Build event each year. These are all shared activities that have come about organically, based on people's interests and talents. We want to enjoy our time at work, since work and life are so closely connected in architecture.

FIGURE 3. Clustered around central project tables, design teams use a variety of techniques to develop their projects. Photography courtesy of Studio Gang.

MC For me, being an architect and being a mother are the two essential and inseparable parts of myself; one informs the other. Figuring out and balancing these two roles has not been easy, but it's been very fulfilling—my perspective on architecture is shaped by my experiences outside the office, and my life outside the office is shaped by my experiences as an architect. It says something about the Studio that we are so supportive of that work-life balance.

JG We encourage people to pursue their own path, to figure it out for themselves, and not to conform to the way it's always been done. I always wanted to be an architect. But once I entered professional practice, I realized I had to remake architecture into what I wanted it to be. It wasn't always what I had in mind. I was driven to start Studio Gang as soon as I possibly could to change the way that practice is done.

MC If something doesn't work the way you want it to work, change it. Figure out how to make it better in a way that navigates around the roadblocks.

JG I don't dwell on roadblocks. I spend time thinking about what I want and how to get it done. Of course, there can be difficulties, but they're often the seeds of solutions. In design,

we continually encounter instances when people say that something can't be done, and that's exactly when it starts to become interesting—and fun. That's a big part of our design process.

MC I mentioned actionable idealism, which is a way that we practice very conscientiously. It's a way of thinking about our work that I find very refreshing.

JG Bringing up a word like "idealism" is tricky because it has so many associations. But for us, actionable idealism describes a very basic impulse to design in a way that's good for the world—for people, communities, cities, and the planet. That's why it's idealistic, because we want to make a difference. And actionable, because we want to see the results and participate in the results.

MC It's about measured steps. With the Arcus Center for Social Justice Leadership at Kalamazoo College, we began by asking, what is social justice? How do you design for it? How do you build for it? What does it look like? So much of social justice work occurs hidden from sight. We knew the architecture had to make the work clear and present. It needed to be open and accessible. So, one of the key steps

in that project was not just following ADA requirements, but making it an example of universal design. We ended up with an architecture that is equitable and flexible. It supports different types of convening, from one-on-one conversations to large symposiums. And it's intuitive—it's clearly and easily accessible. The urban design makes that area of the campus much easier for everyone to navigate. It was a great success and has inspired the college to implement universal design in other projects on campus regardless of project types in order to make spaces that are more just and that bring diverse people together. Each of our projects has some version of taking measured steps that bring about change.

JG The key is to focus the firm's creative energy on projects where we can move the needle on an issue. Sometimes it's inherent to the project type, like the Arcus Center. Sometimes it emerges from the desires of the client. But it's not just responding to a brief—there's a purposefulness upfront. Our boathouses on the Chicago River are a good example of this, having started as a self-initiated research project, which eventually became a book we titled, *Reverse Effect*. The key insight was that increasing people's access to the river would lead to greater stewardship of this natural resource, as well as result in important community and economic benefits. Publishing the book introduced these ideas into the public conversation, and soon after we were able to pursue them with the City of Chicago, who asked us to design two public boathouses—one on the river's North Branch and the other on its South Branch. Seeing the impact that the boathouses have made on the community's ability to use and enjoy the river has been very exciting. It's the

FIGURE 4. Participating in Habitat for Humanity's Women Build program has become a favorite Studio activity. Photography courtesy of Studio Gang.

first step we envisioned that will lead to bigger change.

As you said, Margaret, the Arcus Center presented the opportunity to really explore what it means for a space, for a design, to be just. We learned a lot about how to create spaces that bring diverse groups of people together, and we've been able to apply those insights in subsequent work. It becomes a lens to view all of our projects, especially those at the scale of the city. There is really interesting work being done right now on the equitable, just city. It's a new frontier for design.

MC And a fundamental part of our growing urban design work is community engagement—we've been building our skills through office-wide workshops as well as through the projects themselves.

JG That's a very important part of how our practice is evolving, and it really addresses the question of different lenses and diversity. Engaging the public—which we do in different ways, depending on the project—is a way of breaking down the distance between the designer and the project, so that we're in the mix with others rather than applying our own creative inspiration in isolation. It allows the design to arise and emerge out of multiple vectors of influence, and it's a technique that works at different levels. It helps produce content for designers to react to and work with, and it also helps build support for a project within the community. It's a process that recognizes that there are many different relationships at play. Something I've learned through the engagement process is that an essential part of design is enhancing, adjusting, and supporting networks of relationships. This is a realization architects might not come to if they don't engage directly with the people who have the most at stake in a project. Without that engagement, it's an abstract design exercise.

MC It's much more removed.

JG Making community engagement a major part of the design process puts social relationships at the center—identifying them, observing them, reacting to them, and trying to make them stronger and more enduring. That's the goal of this work.

MC And building relationships, whatever form that takes. Person to person, network to network. You learn things you didn't know along the way and that makes your work better—it makes the project better—and it knits things together to make actionable idealism work.

JG It's been exciting to see how spaces we design are engendering new and stronger relationships. With the Campus North Residential Commons at the University of Chicago, the site was previously closed to the surrounding neighborhood with a twelve-foot-high brick wall. By understanding the desired relationships between the neighborhood and campus communities, which was a desire to connect and convene, we were able to physically link them with a new pathway—an inviting, welcoming portal between the college and the neighborhood, which is really influencing the way people interact with each other. It's a mixing chamber between neighborhood residents, students, and faculty—a place where people are encountering each other in

an informal setting. It's a simple design element that creates and supports the opportunity for these relationships. But we wouldn't have come up with it abstractly, if we hadn't put relationships and social connectivity at the center of the project. We could only arrive there through observing and understanding, talking and engaging, and receiving feedback.

MC We've been building our skills in this area through workshops in the Studio, learning how to engage different people, and drawing from the knowledge and practice of community organizing. It's very interesting work, thinking about how you listen to and speak with another person, how you join them in conversation, and come to where they are. We may think that we know how to do this, but it's something that has to be practiced.

JG It's a technique that we can add to our toolbox along with our other design skills.

MC We're always practicing, whether it's with community members, clients, or with each other in the Studio. Having conversations where everyone is truly heard and encouraged to contribute—it's a key part of building relationships, especially across differences. It isn't easy. You have to work at it. But the rewards are certainly worth it.

FIGURE 6. The Arcus Center for Social Justice Leadership's gently arcing wood masonry walls create a welcoming public space on the Kalamazoo College campus. Photography by Steve Hall © Hedrich Blessing.

PennDesign Women in Architecture hosted two major symposiums in the Spring of 2017 and 2018 at the University of Pennsylvania. These symposiums, centered around the cultivation of visibility and voice, worked to identify the current state of the profession both in academia and practice, and served to equip participants with the information and tools they would need to excel within the field.

[RE]

WHEN Spring 2017

WHERE Penn Design – University of Pennsylvania

WHAT Coalescing students, faculty members, and professionals in architecture, this international symposium centered around understanding the framework, fallout, and future of women in design. From tracing the history of women in the field, understanding their trajectory from graduate school to the gap which occurs in the workplace, and hearing from inspiring female practitioners, the symposium strove to celebrate successful women while understanding the cultural shifts which have continued to perpetuate how women practice.

The Framework, Fallout, and Future of Women in Design

FORM

WHO

The event was organized by students of Penn Design Women in Architecture. It was moderated by Joan Ockman, senior lecturer, Department of Architecture; Daniela Fabricius, Department of Architecture, PennDesign; and Franca Trubiano, associate professor of Architecture, PennDesign.

Presentations by Vanessa Keith, Ila Berman, Lori Brown, Mary McLeod, Danielle Di Leo Kim, Despina Stratigakos, Annelise Pitts, Marilyn Jordan Taylor, Margaret Cavenagh, Winka Dubbeldam, Shirley Blumberg, and Nicole Dosso.

Keynote Address by Marion Weiss, Graham Professor of Architecture, PennDesign.

WHY

The ultimate goal of the symposium was to cultivate understanding and foster action. By examining the historical framework of women in architecture, tracing their educational development to their professional career, and understanding the "gap" which occurs from education to practice, the symposium strove to identify the current cultural climate and identified strategies which help women succeed.

Empowering the Future Leaders in Design

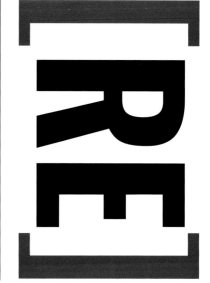

WHEN Spring 2018

WHERE Penn Design–University of Pennsylvania

WHAT [RE]FORM was a full day symposium empowering the future leaders in design. As a part II of [Re]Form in the spring of 2017, [Re]Action took a more hands-on and personalized approach to helping students and young professionals gain valuable knowledge on how to leverage resources and a support network to take charge of their futures. The chosen topics were areas in which students and young professionals felt least comfortable with when starting and preparing for their careers.

WHO The morning portion was a panel titled "Navigating The Design Field + Entrepreneurship". Panelists included Andrew Wit, architect and co-founder of WITO*, Anne Papageorge, landscape architect and vice president of Facilities and Real Estate Services at the University of Pennsylvania, Elizabeth Mahon, architect and managing principal of HDR, Franca Trubiano, architect and associate professor at Penn Design Architecture, Misako Murata, architect, landscape architect, and co-founder of LMNOP, and Tina Delia, interior designer and co-founder of Delia Designs.

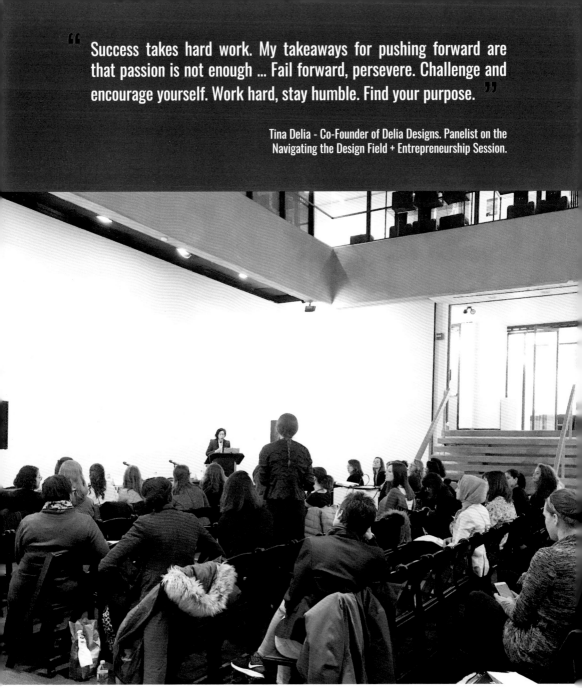

" Success takes hard work. My takeaways for pushing forward are that passion is not enough ... Fail forward, persevere. Challenge and encourage yourself. Work hard, stay humble. Find your purpose. "

Tina Delia - Co-Founder of Delia Designs. Panelist on the Navigating the Design Field + Entrepreneurship Session.

WHY Participants shared a wide range of experiences and expertise offering great examples for students who are pursuing similar passions and interests. The afternoon included a series of workshops that addressed a number of specific skills of value to a career in design and construction. Workshops included: Negotiating Offers, Vocal Empowerment, Navigating Construction Sites, Knowing Your Rights, and Networking for Impact. While the workshops were a great opportunity for networking and for forming connections between the school and area professionals, they also increased awareness of what the profession has to offer. All told, the day's activities further extended the outreach mission of Penn Design Women in Architecture.

> " There are no hierarchies in collaboration. Work with everyone, especially those with different perspectives. "

Andrew Wit - Architect and co-founder of WITO, Panelist on the
Navigating the Design Field + Entrepreneurship Session.

Pictured from left to right: Franca Trubiano, Aahana Miller, Ramona Adlakha, Aishwarya Katta, Rose Deng, Alexa Sternberger, Rebeca Sanchez, Marta Llor, Caitlin Dashiell, Ramune Bartuskaite, and Susan Kolber.

Photography by April Huang, Ericka Lu, and Adrian Subagyo. Courtesy of PennDesign Women in Architecture.

CONTRIBUTORS

Ramona Adlakha Ramona Adlakha lives in Toronto, Canada, and practices architecture at Diamond Schmitt Architects. She was born in Calcutta, India, speaks five languages, and has been lucky enough to call multiple places across the globe her home. Ramona holds a Master of Architecture from the University of Pennsylvania where she received the Alpha Ro Chi Medal for professional promise and the Will M. Melhorn Scholarship in architectural history and theory. Ramona holds a Bachelor of Arts in Architecture, Fine Art, and Literary Studies from the University of Toronto where she was the recipient of the Government of Canada's Millennium Provincial Laureate scholarship awarded for exhibited excellence in community involvement, innovation, and leadership. Ramona has completed architectural study abroad programs at the Architectural Association School of Architecture in London, U.K., and the University of Siena, Italy. She is a founding member of PennDesign Women in Architecture at the University of Pennsylvania, an executive member of Building Equality in Architecture Toronto (BEAT)—a national movement across Canada promoting equity in design, a board member of the Penn-Wharton Club of Toronto, and a LEED accredited professional. Ramona is deeply committed to promoting the visibility and voice of women in design.

Ramune Bartuskaite Ramune Bartuskaite holds a Masters of Architecture from the University of Pennsylvania and a Bachelor of Arts in Architecture with a minor in Marketing from Miami University. During her studies, she also had the privilege of participating in exchange programs in Copenhagen, Denmark, and the Architectural Association School of Architecture in London, U.K. At Penn, she co-founded PennDesign Women in Architecture and was a recipient of the Alpha Rho Chi Medal for leadership, willing service, and promise of professional merit. As a Lithuanian immigrant and a first-generation graduate, Ramune is fascinated by the urban environment, which is home to people of various backgrounds, socio-economic statuses, and agendas. She practices architecture at JKRP Architects in Philadelphia and serves as chief creative director of Rise First—a non-profit for first-generation students. She is actively involved in Urban Land Institute (ULI) Philadelphia and serves as co-chair of the Women's Leadership Initiative. She's a LEED Green Associate, a member of the Building Industry Association (BIA) Philadelphia Green Committee, and Philadelphia's Green Building United and hopes to be an advocate for more equitable, diverse, and inclusive development within our cities.

Ila Berman Ila Berman, dean of the School of Architecture and Edward E. Elson Professor of Architecture at the University of Virginia, and principal of Scaleshift design, is an architect, theorist, and curator of architecture and urbanism whose research and design work investigates the relationship between culture and the evolution of contemporary material, technological, and spatial practices. Dr. Berman's work and publications include *Expanded Field: Architectural Installation Beyond Art*; *FLUX: Architecture in a Parametric Landscape*; *URBANbuild local_global*; and *New Constellations New Ecologies*, among others. She is also the creator of "New Orleans: Urban Operations for a Future City" an exhibition at the 2006 International Architectural Biennale in Venice, Italy; "WBA3: Architecture in the Expanded Field" at the Wattis Institute for Contemporary Arts in San Francisco; and "Urban Syncopation" an installation for Nuit Blanche at the Gardiner Museum in Toronto.

Shirley Blumberg Shirley Blumberg is a founding partner of KPMB Architects in Toronto, and has been appointed to the Order of Canada for her contribution to the field of architecture. Her portfolio ranges from affordable housing to highly specialized cultural and academic institutions, many with a focus on revitalizing heritage contexts. Award-winning projects include Canada's National Ballet School, the Gardiner Museum and Fort York Public Library in Toronto, the CIGI Campus in Waterloo, and the Robert H. Lee Alumni Centre at the University of British Columbia. Recently she was partner-in-charge of the Remai Modern Art Gallery of Saskatchewan, the Ronald O. Perelman Center for Political Science and Economics at the University of Pennsylvania, 20 Washington Road at Princeton University, and the Global Centre for Pluralism in Ottawa for his Highness the AGA Khan. She has served on several design and advisory panels in Toronto, and, in addition to her practice, is a founder of Building Equality in Architecture Toronto (BEAT).

Lori Brown

Lori Brown's creative practice focuses on the relationships between architecture and social justice issues with particular emphasis on gender and its impact upon spatial relationships. She is the co-founder and leads ArchiteXX, www.architexx. org, a women and architecture group in New York City. Her two books include *Feminist Practices: Interdisciplinary Approaches to Women in Architecture*, an edited collection of a group of international women designers and architects employing feminist methodologies in their creative practices, and *Contested Spaces: Abortion Clinics, Women's Shelters and Hospitals,* exploring highly securitized spaces and the impact of legislation and the First Amendment's affect upon such places. She is working with two abortion clinics on design interventions for their public interface. Her two current book projects include *Birthing Centers, Borders and Bodies,* and she is co-editing *The Bloomsbury Global Encyclopedia of Women in Architecture 1960-2015* with Dr. Karen Burns. Through ArchiteXX she is also currently collaborating with the Australian group Parlour and the German group N-Ails to write more women architects into Wikipedia through a Wikipedia Foundation Grant. She is a professor of architecture at Syracuse University and a registered architect in the state of New York.

Margaret Cavenagh

Architect and designer Margaret Cavenagh, AIA, is principal of interior architecture at Studio Gang. Guided by expert observations of how people use space as well as a deep interest in craft and custom fabrication, Margaret has designed dozens of spaces for the Studio that range across scales and types. Her AIA award-winning work includes single-family residences (the Brick Weave House and Maisonette), workspaces (the Midwest headquarters of the Natural Resources Defense Council), educational buildings (the Arcus Center for Social Justice Leadership and Columbia College Media Production Center), and cultural centers (Writers Theatre). In alignment with Studio Gang's ecological focus, environmental considerations are key to Margaret's work and her interior designs have achieved some of the highest sustainability ratings, including LEED Platinum and Living Building Challenge certification. She holds a Master of Architecture from Washington University in St. Louis and a Bachelor of Science in Architecture from the University of Virginia, where she is currently teaching Professional Practice as an adjunct faculty member.

Nicole Dosso

Nicole Dosso, FAIA, is a gifted practitioner of the technical craft of architecture, an expert in the technical challenges of designing tall buildings on complex urban sites, and a mentor to emerging practitioners. As director of SOM's Technical Department in New York, she leads one of the most important groups of technical specialists in the United States. She served as lead technical coordinator on SOM's projects at the World Trade Center site—7 World Trade Center and One World Trade Center—each of which had significant challenges, and whose successful completion heralded the rebirth of a complex urban area that was destroyed by the 9/11 attacks. Her current work in NYC includes the mixed-use 35 Hudson Yards tower, multiple commercial and residential projects comprising the Manhattan West site, development of the Moynihan Train Hall, Farley Post Office conversion, and the reuse of the Landmark Waldorf Astoria building. In January 2016, for recognition of her notable contributions to the advancement of the profession of architecture, Nicole was elected to The College of Fellows of The American Institute of Architects. Nicole is also an adjunct assistant professor at Columbia Graduate School of Architecture, Planning, and Preservation and serves on the Board of Directors for Professional Women in Construction where she advocates for the Minority and Women Owned-Business Enterprise.

Winka Dubbeldam

Winka Dubbeldam is a seasoned academic and design leader, serving as chair and Miller Professor of Architecture at PennDesign, where she has gathered an international network of innovative research and design professionals. Previously, Professor Dubbeldam oversaw the Post-Professional Degree program for ten years (2003-2013), providing students with innovative design skills, cutting-edge theoretical and technological knowledge, and the analytic, interpretive, and writing skills necessary for a productive and innovative career in the field of architecture. She also taught advanced architectural design studios at Columbia University and Harvard University, among other prestigious institutions. Born in the Netherlands, Dubbeldam has a Master of Architecture from the Institute of Higher Professional Architectural Education, Rotterdam (1990), and a MSAAD from Columbia University (1992). A practicing architect and founder/principal of the New York firm Archi-Tectonics, Dubbeldam is widely known for her award-winning work, recognized as much for its use of hybrid sustainable materials and smart building systems as for its elegance and innovative structures. Archi-Tectonics' work ranges from residential to commercial, from real to virtual, and is realized in urban designs, architectural designs, and installations. The firm's use of hybrid sustainable materials and smart building systems is widely noted and its work is recognized for its elegance and innovative structures.

Jeanne Gang

Architect and MacArthur Fellow Jeanne Gang, FAIA, Int. FRIBA, is the founding principal of Studio Gang. A recipient of the Marcus Prize, Louis I. Kahn Memorial Award, and the National Design Award in Architecture, Jeanne is renowned for a design process that foregrounds the relationships between individuals, communities, and environments. Her work spans scales and typologies, from cultural and public buildings to urban plans and high-rise towers. Her analytical and creative approach has resulted in some of today's most award-winning architecture, including the Arcus Center for Social Justice Leadership at Kalamazoo College in Kalamazoo, Michigan; Writers Theatre, a professional theater facility in Glencoe, Illinois; and two public Boathouses on the Chicago River. Jeanne is currently designing major projects throughout the Americas and Europe that include the expansion of the American Museum of Natural History in New York City and the new United States Embassy in Brasilia, Brazil. The author of three books on architecture, she is a professor in practice at the Harvard Graduate School of Design.

Samantha Hardingham

Samantha Hardingham (AA Dip 1993) is an architectural writer, editor, and curator. Her most recent and celebrated work is the award-winning, two-volume anthology *Cedric Price Works 1952-2003: A Forward-minded Retrospective* published by the AA/CCA in October 2016. Samantha has a wide-ranging knowledge and understanding of the AA having been a design tutor across all undergraduate years since 2008, and a member of the academic committees and senior management team since 2015. As interim director in 2017-18, she led the AA in a very special year as the school celebrated a centenary of women at the AA and the culmination of the AA XX 100 project. Samantha is now the creative director of brand and business strategy agency, Theseus.

Mary McLeod

Mary McLeod is a professor of architecture at Columbia University, where she teaches architecture history and theory. Her research and publications have focused on the history of the modern movement and on contemporary architecture theory, examining issues concerning the connections between architecture and ideology. She has written extensively on Le Corbusier's architecture and urban planning, and is the editor of and contributor to the book *Charlotte Perriand: An Art of Living*. She is currently co-editing a website on pioneering American women architects. Her essays have appeared in magazines such as *Assemblage, JSAH, Casabella, AA Files,* and *Oppositions,* as well as in books such as *Architecture School, Modern Women, Architectural Theory since 1968, Le parole dell'architettur, Architecture and Feminism,* and *Le Corbusier: An Atlas of Modern Landscapes.*

Sadie Morgan

Sadie Morgan is a founding director of Stirling Prize winning architecture practiced RMM, alongside Alex de Rijke, Philip Marsh, and Jonas Lencer. The studio is recognized for creating innovative, high quality, and socially useful architecture. dRMM's recent high profile projects include Hastings Pier, Trafalgar Place at Elephant & Castle, Maggie's Oldham and Faraday House at the Battersea Power Station. Sadie chairs the Independent Design Panel for High Speed Two and is a commissioner of the National Infrastructure Commission. In 2017 she was appointed as a Mayor's design advocate for the Greater London Authority and is a non-executive director of the Major Project Association. Sadie lectures internationally on the work of dRMM and the importance of infrastructure that connects back to people and place. In 2013 she became the youngest president of the Architectural Association, and in 2016 she was appointed professor at the University of Westminster and awarded an honorary doctorate from London South Bank University. In 2017, she was named New Londoner of the Year at the New London Awards for her work championing the importance of design at the highest political level.

Julie Torres Moskovitz

Julie Torres Moskovitz, AIA, LEED AP, CPHC/CPHT, is founding principal of Fete Nature Architecture. What drives her architecture firm is engagement in community and creating thoughtful and sustainable spaces for all. She teaches environmental technology, design studios at Pratt and Parsons, and a seminar on Eco-Urban Systems at Syracuse University - NYC campus. She is the architect for the first certified NYC Passive House building, which won a 2014 International Passive House Design Award. Working on a passive house project led to her writing a book entitled *The Greenest Home: Superinsulated and Passive House Design* that included eighteen case studies. Her practice focuses on hyper-efficiency and resiliency. In May 2018, she was appointed by the Mayor Bill de Blasio to the New York City Loft Board as a public member. She and her family are Loft Law tenants and she lives and works out of her space. She is a registered architect in New York and New Jersey and is NCARB-certified, a LEED-accredited professional, and a Certified Passive House Consultant and Tradesman (Building Envelope).

Joan Ockman

Joan Ockman is a distinguished senior lecturer at the University of Pennsylvania School of Design and a visiting professor of architecture at Cooper Union and Cornell. She served as director of the Buell Center for the Study of American Architecture at Columbia from 1994 to 2008. She began her career in the mid-1970s at the Institute for Architecture and Urban Studies in New York, where she was an editor of *Oppositions* and other publications. Her writings on architectural history and theory have appeared widely in journals, anthologies, and exhibition catalogs. Among her edited or co-authored books are *The Modern Architecture Symposia, 1962–1966: A Critical Edition* (2014); *Architecture School: Three Centuries of Educating Architects in North America* (2012); *The Pragmatist Imagination: Thinking about Things in the Making* (2000); and the award-winning *Architecture Culture 1943–1968: A Documentary Anthology* (1993). In 2017 she was named a Fellow of the Society of Architectural Historians.

Annelise Pitts

As the research chair of AIASF's Equity by Design committee, Annelise Pitts has led two national surveys on equity in the architectural profession. This research has provided the industry with metrics on diversity within the profession, and has offered insights into the key drivers of firm culture, talent development, and retention. She has spoken about this project in the Bay Area and nationally. She is an associate with Bohlin Cywinski Jackson in New York. In her design work, she has collaborated with clients and interdisciplinary design teams on programmatically complex design and planning projects. Recent projects include the UC Santa Barbara Instructional Hall & Theater, UC Davis Large Lecture Hall, and campus planning for Dominican University of California.

Despina Stratigakos

Despina Stratigakos is University at Buffalo vice provost for Inclusive Excellence and a professor of architecture in the Department of Architecture. She is the author of three books that explore the intersections of power and architecture. Her most recent book, *Where Are the Women Architects?* (2016), confronts the challenges women face in the architectural profession. *Hitler at Home* (2015) investigates the architectural and ideological construction of the Führer's domesticity, and *A Women's Berlin: Building the Modern City* (2008) traces the history of a forgotten female metropolis. Dr. Stratigakos has served as a director of the Society of Architectural Historians, an advisor of the International Archive of Women in Architecture at Virginia Tech, and deputy director of the Gender Institute at the University at Buffalo. She also participated on Buffalo's municipal Diversity in Architecture task force and was a founding member of the Architecture and Design Academy, an initiative of the Buffalo Public Schools to encourage design literacy and academic excellence. She received her Ph.D. from Bryn Mawr College.

Franca Trubiano

Franca Trubiano is an associate professor in Architecture at the University of Pennsylvania and a registered architect with *l'Ordre des Architectes du Québec*. Her edited book *Design and Construction of High-Performance Homes: Building Envelopes, Renewable Energies and Integrated Practice* (Routledge Press, 2012), was translated into Korean and winner of the 2015 Sejong Outstanding Scholarly Book Award. She is presently completing her manuscript *Building Theories* for Routledge, which challenges late 20th-century definitions and practices of architectural theory; and was co-organiser of the spring 2019 symposium "Architectural Theory Now?" held at PennDesign. Franca was president of the Building Technology Educators Society (BTES) (2015); a founding member of the editorial board of the journal *Technology, Architecture and Design* (TAD); and a member of the *Journal of Architectural Education* (JAE) (2013-2016). She has published essays on high-performance design in *Architecture and Energy* (Routledge, 2013) and *Architecture and Uncertainty* (Ashgate, 2014).

Billie Tsien

Billie Tsien along with her partner, Tod Williams, founded their New York City based firm Tod Williams Billie Tsien Architects | Partners in 1986. Their practice is committed to reflecting the values of non-profit, cultural, and academic institutions toward an architecture of permanence and enduring vision. A sense of rootedness, light, texture, detail, and, most of all, experience, are at the heart of what they design. Some of their notable projects include the Barnes Foundation in Philadelphia, Asia Society Center in Hong Kong, and they are currently designing The Obama Presidential Center in Chicago. Over the past three decades, their dedication to this work has been recognized by numerous national and international citations including the National Medal of the Arts from President Obama and the 2013 Firm of the Year Award from the American Institute of Architects. In parallel with her practice, Billie is a devoted participant in the broader cultural community with longstanding associations with many arts organizations. She currently serves as the president of the Academy of Arts and Letters, and was recently the president of the Architectural League of New York (2014-2018). In addition to this she maintains an active academic career and lectures worldwide. As an educator and practitioner she is deeply committed to creating a better world through architecture.

Manijeh Verghese

Manijeh Verghese is an architect of ideas, audiences, and connections. She is interested in the different forms of architectural practice, and the communication of architecture through various media and formats. At the AA, she directs the AA Public Programme, and is the editor of the website AA Conversations. She is a unit master of Diploma 12 and is also a seminar leader for the Architectural Professional Practice for Fifth Year, Part 2 course. From 2015 to 2018, she led a postgraduate design studio at Oxford Brookes University and previously was also a design tutor of AA Intermediate Unit 11. She has worked for architecture practices including John Pawson and Foster + Partners, and has contributed to design publications such as *Disegno* and *Icon*, as well as think-tanks, books and peer reviewed journals.

Marion Weiss

Marion Weiss is the Graham Chair Professor of Architecture at the University of Pennsylvania's School of Design and the co-founder of WEISS/MANFREDI Architecture/Landscape/Urbanism, a multidisciplinary design practice based in New York City. The firm's award-winning projects include the Olympic Sculpture Park, the Women's Memorial at Arlington National Cemetery, Brooklyn Botanic Garden's Visitor Center, Barnard's Diana Center, and Penn's Singh Center for Nanotechnology. Current projects include the U.S. Embassy in New Delhi and a research and development hub for Cornell Tech's groundbreaking new campus on Roosevelt Island in New York City. Weiss has also taught design studios at Harvard University, Cornell University, and was the Eero Saarinen Visiting Professor at Yale University. She has been honored by the Cooper Hewitt, Smithsonian Design Museum with the 2018 National Design Award for Architecture, the AIANY President's Award, the Academy Award for Architecture from the American Academy of Arts and Letters, the Architectural League's Emerging Voices Award, and her work has been exhibited at the Museum of Modern Art, the Venice Architecture Biennale, the Louvre, and the Guggenheim Museum.

Published by Applied Research and Design Publishing, an imprint of ORO Editions.
Gordon Goff: Publisher

www.appliedresearchanddesign.com
info@appliedresearchanddesign.com

Editors: Franca Trubiano, Ramona Adlakha, and Ramune Bartuskaite
With contributions by Joan Ockman, Marion Weiss, Ila Berman, Mary McLeod, Despina Stratigakos, Manijeh Verghese, Sadie Morgan, Samantha Hardingham, Lori Brown, Julie Torres Moskovitz, Annelise Pitts, Billie Tsien, Shirley Blumberg, Nicole Dosso, Winka Dubbeldam, Jeanne Gang, and Margaret Cavenagh.
Book Design by the editors.

Cover photography credits:
Top image: Novartis Visitor Reception. Photography by Albert Vecerka/Esto. Courtesy of Weiss/Manfredi.
Middle image: The Arcus Center for Social Justice Leadership's gently arcing wood masonry walls create a welcoming public space on the Kalamazoo College campus. Photography by Steve Hall © Hedrich Blessing.
Bottom image: The Annenberg Light Court, The Barnes Foundation, 2012, Philadelphia, PA. © Michael Moran

Project Manager: Jake Anderson

10 9 8 7 6 5 4 3 2 1 First Edition

ISBN: 978-1-943532-43-8

Color Separations and Printing: ORO Group Ltd.
Printed in China.

AR+D Publishing makes a continuous effort to minimize the overall carbon footprint of its publications. As part of this goal, AR+D, in association with Global ReLeaf, arranges to plant trees to replace those used in the manufacturing of the paper produced for its books. Global ReLeaf is an international campaign run by American Forests, one of the world's oldest nonprofit conservation organizations. Global ReLeaf is American Forests' education and action program that helps individuals, organizations, agencies, and corporations improve the local and global environment by planting and caring for trees.